If Your
Higher Power
is Jesus

A Christian 12 Step Journey
Through Addiction

M. Kim Son

Potter's Wheel
PRESS

I would like to dedicate this book to: Amy, Sam, Kenny, Mom, Leanne, Judi, Pastor Sandy, and my editor, Laura Dent. In your own unique way, each one of you gave me the priceless gift of encouragement.

Contents

Introduction

I LIVED INSIDE THE WORLD of addiction for forty years.

Most of those forty years I was also a dedicated Christian who just wanted to get it right. Although I avoided calling the "problem" what it actually was, I knew the issue was serious and dearly needed answers. But the answers did not come. As a result, I ran the gauntlet between shame, condemnation, anger, blame, self-pity, disgust, and hopelessness. That all changed, however, on the day I sat in my first Alcoholics Anonymous meeting listening to others share different versions of my story, over and over again. After decades of denial, I finally pulled the veil aside and stared at the unvarnished truth.

I was an addict.

But food, not alcohol, was my drug of choice.

It's amazing how one moment in time can change the course of your entire life, but I had such a moment one Saturday morning in

December of 2013. It led to a supernatural rendezvous of past and present experiences that brought transformation from the inside out. Where once I felt lost and confused, a new light of revelation began to dawn. The chains of bondage floated to the surface like they were made of buoyant plastic, and God started fishing. Some things changed quickly, and others were tied to a long line that had to be reeled in progressively. But the results have been, nonetheless, miraculous. After years of feeling baffled and condemned, a new way of life has emerged.

And the Lord began providing opportunities to share. The leader of one of my support groups invited me to present my experiences using the Twelve Steps, so I launched into a writing project with bi-weekly presentations to the group. It was a gathering of other churchgoing Christians shackled by similar chains as mine. Now, after years of recovery, it seems clear to me that the body of Christ is no more immune to addiction than it is to divorce—all of which makes perfect sense, since both are generated by brokenness. Christians struggle with brokenness as much as anyone, and it seems to me that thousands of believers are stranded in a similar boat of confusion, with no land in sight. They are held captive by addictive substances and behaviors and don't understand why freedom is elusive. Some don't even know that they are addicted.

In response, I believe God has been sending out wake-up calls.

As it happens, my wake-up call came through the Twelve Steps of Alcoholics Anonymous. The Steps are based on scripture, and the godly principles of the Twelve Step program brought a metamorphosis that is absolutely priceless. My hope is that others will follow. But it's not easy. Recovery and discipleship are much alike; they are both about change. And change is seldom easy. My long-term understanding has been that discipleship isn't just about going to church and reading the Bible on occasion. It's about becoming more and more like Jesus through the power of His Spirit and becoming an effective tool in God's hands for the Kingdom. But in order to do that, I have to be willing to look within and become a lump of clay on the Potter's wheel. The first three Steps of the Twelve Step program can turn someone into a lump of clay mighty fast. The fact is: I want to be more like Jesus, and this Program helps me grow into a better reflection of His light and love.

Before we move forward, however, there is a question that may need to be answered.

Some Christians believe that addiction is simply a sin that can be cured by the act of true repentance. On the other hand, folks in Twelve Step call addiction a disease. So, which is it? I can only draw from my own experience, but I have concluded that it's both. Sin *and* sickness. And they both have to be addressed in order for freedom to prevail.

Frankly, it took me quite a while to even consider using the Twelve Steps, largely because of this very question. I was one of those who called addiction a sin, only, and lost count long ago of the number of times I "repented." Falling flat on my face over and over again brought nothing but condemnation. But, although the realization came later, part of the failure was due to a lack of knowledge. I simply did not recognize the sickness in my soul and certainly didn't know how to address the *dis*-ease.

Fortunately, God sent Jesus to heal our hearts and set us free. This book is about traveling down that healing road and discovering a whole new life. I freely admit that there is more than one avenue of healing, and we each have to follow the pathway that works for us as individuals. But for me, God ultimately used the Steps because they have a way of simplifying and clarifying what is so very easy for me to *complicate*. I have an uncanny gift for analyzing something to death, and when I stay "up in my head" too much, it gets me into trouble. What I needed was to get out of my head and take action. I needed to apply godly principles. And as I applied the Twelve Steps with Jesus as my Higher Power, I found the ability to trust along with a proven pathway of healing for my brokenness. The Biblical Twelve Step *principles* of faith, humility, and healthy dependence formed a backbone for change.

If you and I share common struggles, I would like to take you on an intimate journey through the Twelve Steps where you will hopefully find new understanding, compassion, wisdom, and insight. And all from a Christian standpoint. May you glean a word of encouragement and find experience that becomes applicable. May you also catch a glimpse of humanity that resonates with your own. If we each go through our pain and learn the available lessons, then the storytelling becomes worthwhile.

Lastly, I want to share that the words, thoughts, and memories on these pages are my own. They may not perfectly match someone else's memories or perceptions. In fact, I would be immensely surprised if they *did*. But I have taken on the responsibility of dealing with my own reality in the best way I know. The positive end-results far surpass the difficulties, and I'm thankful for the great goodness that has been revealed through the grace of God. I also want to say how grateful I am for my mom and dad. As I look back, the richness they added to my life is clearly evident, and even though my dad is gone now, I dearly love them both. They are priceless treasures that I carry in my heart, always.

[The names of the people mentioned in this book have been changed for the sake of their privacy and personal protection.]

Fairy Tales:
Setting the Stage

THE DESIRE TO RUN AWAY was so strong I could taste it.

For the last seven months, my thoughts and emotions had been one long torment, churning and grinding like the gears in an old pickup. There was nothing smooth about them. They were jagged and ugly and dark, showing up unannounced and unwelcome. Busyness was at least a distraction, but never quite enough. I felt like a desperate animal trying to escape the sights of a big game hunter. I felt stalked. I felt powerless. And all I wanted ... was to feel numb.

No one warned me that it would be like this. Back then, all I could think about was restoring my life to some semblance of normal ... whatever "normal" was. The thought of having the responsibility of a child was overwhelming beyond words. And at the age of seventeen, I felt utterly alone. But the choice I had made went against everything I believed, and "normal" was nowhere to be found. I was strapped into the passenger seat of an out-of-control race car driven by guilt and self-loathing.

I had to make it stop.

There was no question that they were rich, sweet, and forbidden. The first bite was like a shot of heroin to a junkie; the last bite was tasteless and already held the promise of regret. No one should waste French Crullers the way I did that day ... with minimal culinary awareness, crouched behind the bushes in our front yard. But eating did the trick: it shut down the voices, even if only temporarily.

Finding solace in food was not a new thing in my life, but this was the first time the act was totally premeditated. I knew exactly what I was doing. There was no reason to treat myself with kindness. I had every reason to dive headfirst into a downward spiral. So, what had previously been a knee-jerk reaction to sporadic emotional pain became frequent and very intentional.

And that was the beginning of an addiction that took over my life for the next four decades.

I never planned to become an addict. Who does? My dad sure didn't. My granddaddy didn't, and my great-granddaddy didn't. But it happened, nonetheless. While researching our family history, one of my cousins discovered the documentation of alcoholism in every generation going all the way back to the Civil War, with one father after another succumbing to the tyrant. My dad's obsession with alcohol started around 1971, but long before he crossed over the line, our household suffered from the subtle effects of soul-sickness.

Alcoholism takes the normal out of life.

Although Mom and Dad were from families with many positive qualities, they also lived in environments in which affection was rare, rules were strict, standards were high, and criticism was common. My grandparents on both sides were divorced before I was born due to addiction and adultery: soul-sickness.

But they were also hard-working, talented individuals with much to offer. Addicts aren't bad people, and my parents and grandparents were perfect examples of that fact. Mom and Dad were well respected citizens with good intentions and a solid work ethic. Dad was a college graduate, very likable—a fine man in many ways—and I loved him dearly. Mom was a homemaker, a great cook, a gardener, a reader of thought-provoking literature, a lovely woman of great intelligence, and a gifted artist. She still is.

My older brother, four years my senior, was my hero. I adored everything he did and tried to be like him. He always called me Kimmy. My older sister was my absolute opposite. She had a perfect ballerina figure; I felt like a sack of potatoes. She was popular and had lots of friends; I was shy and a loner. She was the "angel" of the family; I was always in trouble. My relationship with her was a tug-of-war between jealousy and admiration. My little brother, who came along almost five years after me, was the adored youngest and my buddy ... in early seasons.

Our family had plenty of enjoyable times together, and I remember playing circus, having basketball games on the driveway, and decorating the Christmas tree for our annual festivities. But for me, those memories were overshadowed by a hazy cloud of confusion. Problems weren't solved. Emotions weren't identified or acknowledged. Affection wasn't shown. Saying, "I love you," was mostly nonexistent. Alcohol was prevalent but never discussed. Verbal affirmations were rare. Perfection was the unspoken standard. Communication was minimal. And listening to the heart of a child was a fine art never mastered.

The mystery of why I felt unloved clothed me like an invisible shroud, but when I was three years old, it became evident that something was wrong. My hair started falling out in large patches, and I ended up partially bald. After several tests, the doctor concluded that the problem was emotional, not physical. My hair eventually grew back, but the emotional distress remained.

And by then, I had discovered the comforts of food.

It was a setup.

The memory of my first recognizable indulgence is crystal clear because, from the very start, I felt this kind of eating was something I needed to hide. There was no specific catalyst, only an urgent and persistent thought that suddenly popped into my head. So, at the age of six, I snuck into the kitchen and, like a mouse in the dark of night, very quietly prepared four slices of bread with a thick "frosting" of butter and sugar ... and ate them outside in the bushes.

Maybe it was because I felt depressed. Maybe it was because I almost died that summer and thought my parents didn't care. Maybe it was just because the Enemy of Our Souls is always looking for an opportunity to steal, kill, and destroy. I don't know. But it does seem a bit diabolical that such ugly thoughts and feelings would be planted in the heart of a child. Unfortunately, it happens every day, in every nation, in every corner of the world.

The point is: my life didn't get off to a wonderful start.

And it's also true that a plethora of good was interwoven into the fabric of those days, months, and years. It wasn't all bad. And maybe that's because I also had a Lover of My Soul who watched over me, even though I had only an inkling of who He was. In the face of death, He reached out His hand and miraculously saved me. In the midst of depression, I found a sensitivity to the pain of others. In solitude, I discovered the beauty of nature. And in loneliness, there was the richness of an inner imagination.

Indeed, I can look back and see His hand at every turn. I didn't know Him then, but my instincts told me that there was a powerful, benevolent, and invisible Being out there. I became quietly determined to find Him. But, first, I had to live a little more of life.

So ... my younger years were filled with the vague sensation of something being "off kilter" with our family. In a movie scene from *Two Weeks Notice*, Hugh Grant says it very well. As he is unknowingly eating a piece of cake made totally out of tofu, a puzzled expression crosses his face. With his lips slightly twisted and mouth half full, he stops chewing and says to Sandra Bullock, "Something is amuck with this cake."[1] Bingo.

Something was amuck at our house. I just didn't know what to call it.

Unfortunately, my response to this unease was to try to get attention in any way I could, which turned out to be mostly negative. At home, I was defiant and in trouble much of the time. My relationship with Mom was something more than uncomfortable. I remember a lot of glaring looks and daggered criticisms. I think she loved me, but I don't think she liked me. I was her problem child. I found myself despising her sharp words of correction and simultaneously longing for her approval, which rarely came.

But I could hear the affirmation in her voice when she commented on my piano playing. She loved music, and I could make our old upright sing when I set my mind to it. At the end of a soulful sonata, or the ebb and flow of a piece like Claire de Lune, she would comment on its beauty and how well I played. I lived for such moments. Her words were a small respite from the plague of rejection that manifested elsewhere: with siblings, playmates, schoolmates, so-called friends, and a boyfriend or two in later years. Rejection was real and consistent. I could imagine it, create it, wallow in it, look for it, bathe in it, and dish it out even when I was completely oblivious to my ability to do so. But at some point, I became deathly afraid of it. Rejection was the tool of torment, but fear itself became my arch enemy.

So, in the midst of fear and anxiety, I ate.

And I ate.

And I ate.

Food was wonderful. It made me feel happy and comfortable and loved. It helped me forget. It covered up the pain. It became my friend. My really good friend ... right up until the moment I opened my physical fitness report in Mr. Ramsey's sixth-grade classroom. That spring, my physical education teacher indicated with a strategically placed check mark that I was "possibly overweight." That simple check mark hit me like a stun gun from an episode of Star Trek. I was horrified. I was appalled.

I was FAT.

And the label stuck.

At least in my mind.

That was not my teacher's intention—just my reaction. But that which had once been my good friend suddenly became my enemy.

The truth was: I was overweight, but I was way too active and burned off too many calories to be obese at that point. Nonetheless, I promptly went on my first diet, consisting of a bowl of peaches and cottage cheese three times a day. As you can imagine, it didn't last long. So, I researched, experimented, and settled on calorie counting to take off the pounds. It worked. And I got so thin that my mom thought I was seriously ill. But as far as I was concerned, being overweight meant that I was unlovable, and rejection would be the unavoidable result. Consequently, fear took over, along with an obsession to be thin.

That's how I commenced my middle school years—years which became an emotional roller coaster with no end. As for the weight, my slender "glory days" were short-lived, and I eventually regained the pounds, and then some. I also made the unwelcome discovery that girls can be mean for no reason at all. Experiencing so much angst by the beginning of ninth grade, I vowed to be a loner, at least until I ended up discovering boys and had my first serious boyfriend. This turned into a series of unhealthy attachments where I made each successive boyfriend the sum total of my existence. So, in the blink of an eye, I projected myself into the world of codependency.

That's where I was when my granddaddy died.

His alcoholism had advanced to where he was getting drunk in public on a frequent basis. But early one morning in May of 1970, the phone rang just after the sun came up. Having been awakened, I went in to investigate and watched the color drain out of my dad's face when he learned his father had suffered a blow to the head causing a cranial hemorrhage.

Granddaddy was dead.

And no one knew how it happened.

I was fifteen years old at the time, and Granddaddy was my first close family member to die. His death, and the unusual circumstances, left a gaping hole that just exacerbated my need to escape. So, along with the food battle and the obsession with my weight, I was also spending an unusual amount of time fantasizing about the most wonderful guy in the world who would sweep me off my feet, marry me, and help me create the perfect family in which I would live happily ever after.

Fairy tales.

I was looking for an all-consuming love that would be the answer to all my problems and alleviate all my pain. I believed. And, in essence, I wasn't completely wrong.

Not long after Granddaddy died, my dad slid from alcohol abuse into alcoholism. And there is a difference. He was also the local Don Juan and apparently had quite the reputation in certain circles. His flirtations and affairs were well known, and to say it politely, I found his lifestyle deeply disturbing. Since problems weren't discussed at our house, I didn't know where or how to share my thoughts and feelings, so I felt very much alone.

Until Danny came along.

As seniors in high school, we discovered each other via our assigned seats in A Capella Choir. There was a definite spark. He liked me just the way I was. We had lots of fun together, and his arm around my shoulder felt like a warm blanket on a cold winter night. We felt safe with each other and were both children of alcoholics, which seemed to create an instant bond. But the summer after we graduated, we got involved physically, and I became pregnant. When we decided to get married, my dad was silent, and my mom went ballistic. She suggested getting an abortion instead. At first, I was horrified, but over the next several weeks, I became more and more afraid of being trapped in a marriage and in parenthood for which I was completely unprepared.

In the end ... I agreed.

It was done out of town in a Catholic hospital, and the nurses knew why I was there. They did not hide the fact that they thought I was despicable. Before surgery, I was placed in a room with a woman whose baby had just been stillborn, and the woman cried all night long. Thankfully, she never knew my reason for admittance. The next morning, my scheduled procedure was done, and after a few hours of recovery, my parents took me home.

I was seventeen and had lost my innocence, spirit, soul, and body. It would have been a relief for someone to just crush me like a bug and be done with it. And looking into Danny's face brought overwhelming guilt and shame. He understood the breakup even less than I did. So, at that point, the need for an effective distraction bobbed to the surface like a bloated dead frog in a pond. The alcohol in the corner cupboard of our kitchen had never been a big draw before, but I started in with coke and shots of bourbon. That went on intermittently for about two months until I had an opportunity to "take a good look in the mirror" ... and stopped cold turkey.

But four months later, in the month that the baby would have been born, I had my first premeditated food binge: the French Crullers. At the time, I never would have called it suicide, but that's what it was. The method was just long, slow, and insidious. I didn't go for something like carbon monoxide, a bullet to the head, or a drug overdose. I went for something legal, easy to buy, and unhurried in its power to destroy.

After that, bingeing became a frequent escape—something I loved and despised at the same time. I loved it because it provided temporary relief; then I hated myself because I couldn't stop. Two years later, when I was twenty years old, Mom shared a story with me that began to shed some new light. During the time of her pregnancy with me, she was emotionally devastated by my dad's interest and possible affair with a woman at his workplace. When I was born, she cared for my physical needs but didn't have anything else to give. She was empty. As she was reciting her story that day, I realized that somehow her emptiness had been transferred to me in the womb and afterward as well. The knowledge of that incident helped pull together a few puzzle pieces, but unfortunately, it did not alter my negative course.

I was, however, strangely drawn to the Bible. And after seventeen months of reading, searching, and "coincidentally" running into Christians eager to share their stories, God supernaturally brought someone across my path who prayed with me to receive Jesus in my heart.

Life changed direction, and the depression, which had become clinical, miraculously disappeared. But I was still bingeing on occasion, even though I tried valiantly to make a different choice. Since my only knowledge of how to live life was performance based, I worked very hard to do everything right in my Christian walk. I was trying to earn God's love and approval, not realizing that I was nullifying His grace. I really had no clue that I had transferred the old mode of operation into this new season, relying on my own strength in the process. So, I failed over and over again.

Amidst a cloud of disillusionment during my senior year in college, I completely lost focus and dropped out. And returning back home to live with my parents felt like a giant step backward. But I realize now that, emotionally, I was acting out my "age." I was still very young. The days turned into monotony working at a local bank, with a change of pace to be found only in the excitement of the little church I discovered. There was joy and a supernatural element in that place that was invigorating; it fed my spiritual hunger. One Sunday night at church, I had a special experience with God in which I felt called to devote my life to full-time ministry. From that moment on, I began to prepare. I wasn't sure what that ministry was going to look like, but it became my life's purpose.

Meanwhile, for almost three years, I had been dating a young man named Jason who also felt called to ministry. We got married in May of 1976, then proceeded to get pregnant on our honeymoon, having our first child, a daughter, nine months later. I was twenty-two years old.

Within two years, Jason and I had both attended a local Bible college and launched a short-lived teaching ministry where he taught, and I led musical worship. But I was also a struggling new mom, emotionally immature to the extreme and five years into compulsive bingeing. In fact, by that time the bingeing had escalated to an alarming degree. It was nothing for me to eat the entire contents of a large bag of flavored corn chips, a large bag of licorice twists, and two or three fried pastry rolls with chocolate or caramel icing. In one sitting. Then I would fall asleep on the couch as my blood sugar spiked and bottomed out. I did all this while my husband was at work and our daughter was taking a three-hour afternoon nap.

I was starting to wonder if I had a serious problem ...

In the spring of 1978, I added romance books to my routine. (Now, watch the pattern.) I could mentally and emotionally escape into a fictional world where I was thin, beautiful, hard-working, courageous, and being pursued by the perfect man. Cinderella lives. It was a very powerful ninety-nine cent relief, and it only took a few months for me to get totally hooked; a second addiction added to my hall of shame.

It may sound totally ridiculous that I was moving toward full-time ministry, but I was in complete denial about the sickness in my life. I knew my behaviors were wrong, but each episode was followed by remorse and a plea for forgiveness. And each day I woke up in a cloud of self-deception, believing I would never do it again and all would be well.

Fairy Tales:
The Quagmire

BY 1979, MY DAD'S DRINKING had become blatantly destructive, so our family did an intervention and off to rehab he went. It didn't stick, however, and he soon went back to the vodka. My mom started talking divorce at that point, and she even filed once, but didn't go through with it. By then I was disgusted with both of them and tried, unsuccessfully, to wash my hands of the whole mess.

Our second child, a son, was born soon thereafter. He was only sixteen months old when Jason and I packed up the kids and moved to Texas to receive more ministry training. Then, in 1983, we felt directed to move to Washington D.C. to start a church. It was a family-centered church with a commission from God to pray for the government. Jason was the lead pastor, teacher, and administrative head. I was the worship leader and women's ministry leader, and I also taught frequently in our services. We started with seven people in a hotel room in a Washington, D.C. suburb, and nine years later, it had grown to four hundred. It was exciting, and we felt we were where God wanted us to be, doing what God wanted us to do. But the truth was: we were two people who had simply made ourselves available—not two people who were qualified and equipped to sustain a fruitful ministry.

It was a roller coaster ride.

And I was ill-prepared for the hardships that came in all different forms. My mind held the knowledge of God's Word, but it was a mental ascent instead of a vibrant, living faith. So, I was still operating in my own strength and dealing with anxiety every day of my life. The addictions remained, with indulgences occurring whenever I could do them "secretly." Like, God couldn't see me.

Nor was my daughter blind to what was happening.

She was old enough to be aware that I was sometimes "layering" a romance book behind a larger book that was "acceptable for me to read" in an effort to hide what I was doing. No one seemed to know, however, that a stash of candy and chips was frequently under the little round table next to my reading chair. My place of devouring. Romance books and binge food, both. The table was covered with a floor-length tablecloth that formed a "cave" big enough to hold my bounty. Those were not pleasant years. Our son was young enough to bypass some of the hard realities, but our daughter got caught in the middle. Addictions are isolating by nature, so I was physically there in the home but "gone" in many respects. Not every single day ... but often enough. With my "absence," my daughter became a pseudo-parent and a caretaker for her brother on a part-time basis, and her childhood was cut short. It was like being constantly "on call," and she never knew when she would be on or off duty. Mine was the sin of self-absorption and neglect, and in that difficult season, my kids had about half of a mom ... and it wasn't an especially good half. The tragic irony is that the very thing that created my own emotional damage led to my repeating the "crime."

In my years of recovery, listening to the stories of so many others, this destructive pattern has shown itself over and over again. Some of us even swore that we would be different—that what our parents did, we would never do. But that which is unhealed, remains, and we are destined to repeat the injury by default. My parents weren't trying to hurt me; they were repeating their injuries by default. Likewise, my offenses were not done in hatred or on purpose; but that didn't keep them from causing harm.

This was to become a razor-edged reality—one that I would eventually have to face.

But the greatest blessing of those years was coming into my calling. The music and teaching gifts God had planted inside me had opportunity to grow and develop into something useful and productive. And in that respect, it was a season of pure delight. What can be more satisfying than stepping into what you were created to be and do? I have not found its equal anywhere else, nor is there any expectation of doing so. It's quite evident that God made us to find true fulfillment in doing His will, and in spite of the overwhelming challenges of those years, there is absolutely no regret in that part of the journey.

And five years into that journey, I actually experienced four wonderful months of sobriety. It was a taste of freedom that whetted my appetite for more, but I relapsed back into the food and books and paid the price of unbearable shame. The pain became strong motivation to seek help at my first Twelve Step meeting. At that point, it had taken thirteen years of failure in the hallways of my Christian walk to bring me to a place of honesty about my condition. That, in itself, is a testimony to the strength of denial in the midst of addiction. And, truthfully, I wasn't actually free from the denial, but the chains had loosened.

Looking back, at least in my life, it seems that every season holds a mixture of joy and pain. I have not yet been immersed in either one exclusively. Usually, for various reasons, there is more of one than the other, but even in the middle of dire straits, I have always had elements of joy to embrace. And, in times of happiness, there have also been painful components in the wings. Maybe that's just the nature of living in this earth.

So, after fifteen years of bingeing, it may come as no surprise that my body was beginning to rebel. When I returned to the addiction after the four-month hiatus, it was as though all "junk food" had become poisonous to my system. My digestion was completely messed up, almost nonfunctioning, and distressing symptoms developed. Without being indelicate, let's just say my body kept trying to expel the poisons. And yet, I didn't, or couldn't stop the compulsive eating. I tried everything I knew, but to no avail.

You'd think my lightning-fast brain would have figured out that something was missing ... but what can I say? I was still mostly clueless. I had been locked into the belief that becoming a Christian was the answer to every problem I had and that "performance" in my

Christian life would eventually produce the desired results. What were the desired results? I'm not sure I knew. I think I was still focused on "losing weight." And even though the bingeing and romance book reading were creating deficits—mentally, emotionally, socially, physically, and spiritually, I really had not identified those choices as addictions by the time 1988 rolled around. They were sin, to be sure, but not addictions. Nor did going to Twelve Step meetings such as Overeaters Anonymous truly convince me that I was an addict. I thought I just had a "problem" that needed to be overcome, even if that meant going to a Twelve Step support group where Jesus wasn't necessarily the "Higher Power of choice." He was my Higher Power, and I was not alone in that choice, but it was quite a leap for me to even venture into this kind of setting. Until then, my thinking had been very narrow, rigid, and protected by walls of religious teachings.

I want to make it clear that I totally believe in the power and truth of God's Word. But back in those days, I was hearing the Bible through dysfunctional filters; filters created by my unhealthy perceptions of life and relationships. Consequently, my beliefs were a bit skewed and faulty in application; I simply was not getting the promised power and freedom. It was baffling to me, to say the least.

The other somewhat "amazing" element was my complete lack of knowledge in regard to emotional healing. When God quietly spoke to me one day that He wanted to be my "emotional healer," my response was ... "Huh?"

I had no idea what that meant. But He did. And 1988 was the start of that healing process, even though it was at a tortoise pace. While continuing my attendance at support groups, I also began to study books on emotional healing and looked past the maze of negativity in my life to what might lay underneath. It was scary territory indeed. But despair can often be the engine that powers us into change.

In July of 1991, the Lord used a particular scripture to give me the shot of spiritual adrenaline that I needed. As that scripture "jumped off the page," I knew that God was promising to see me through every aspect of the emotional healing in front of me; He was making it clear that all I had to do was cooperate by doing my part, and He would make sure it got done right. That was no small thing for me. So, that day, I stepped across the starting line into the marathon race of my life.

And I have never looked back.

Along with a significant amount of self-study concerning the alcoholic family system, I attended support groups for children of alcoholics, as well as a weekly session with a wonderful Christian counselor. For the first time, I opened up a lot of dark closets with another human being, finding love and acceptance instead of the feared rejection. I was doing a Fourth and Fifth Step and didn't know it at the time, but it changed my life. I received forgiveness and healing for the abortion, released large chunks of anger and resentment toward my parents, and began to see myself and others from a new viewpoint.

I also started passing on helpful information to both of our kids whenever it seemed appropriate. In an effort to educate them about self-awareness and healing, I shared some of my personal discoveries and God's pathways to peace. We explored the world of recognizing emotions and the components of a healthy relationship. Most of what I shared was book knowledge with a little experience thrown in, but I felt a strong desire to give them something as a springboard from dysfunction to a better way of living.

The bingeing, however, continued. I was still trying to quit on my own. I would get so frustrated, and at times the self-hatred was so deep, that I thought about suicide ... something "quick and easy." I still, obviously, didn't know how to trust God, and the increasing physical problems were adding to the distress and growing hopelessness.

Meanwhile, after thirteen years in D.C., our church went through a split; our associate pastor left the church and about 40 percent of the congregation went with him. And, simultaneously, our marriage was falling apart. My addictions, and my husband's, were not fertile ground for successful ministry or genuine love, either one. We were both extremely fearful and controlling. With all the pain, and the inability to deal with the circumstances, I started making plans to leave. My husband's frame of mind and emotions were such that he agreed the kids and I should go, although he undoubtedly thought it would only be temporary. So, I left the marriage, left the ministry, and went back to Kansas. My husband and I eventually let go of the church and tried to reconcile over a period of two and a half years, but the efforts were fruitless, and we were divorced by December of 1998.

...And that is the really short version.

I wish I could say at this point that I hit bottom, found a new trust in God, and got set free from bondage. But it wasn't yet time. One of the hallmarks of recovery is to come to the place where you can be grateful for every moment of your life history, knowing that each of those moments had to be experienced in order to bridge the gap between captivity and freedom. I wasn't anywhere close to that space.

I was, however, ready to begin to move toward it.

Back in Kansas, my parents were still married, but my dad was also still drinking. He had attended Alcoholics Anonymous meetings and had experienced a full year of sobriety in the mid-eighties, but once again, it didn't stick, and the obsession returned. Meanwhile, I began the slow process of finally growing up. That included full-time employment at a community college, finishing a bachelor's degree, and walking with my young adult children through the stages of grief over the loss of our family unit as well as the church. At the time, I didn't know how to process that pain much better than they, so we stumbled through it, together and separately, as time and proximity allowed. Even to this day, on certain occasions, we end up in discussions about the demise of our family as we had known it. Their relationship with their dad wasn't good to begin with, and so far, significant improvements have not been made over time. So, they have been left dealing with unresolved issues from a one-sided viewpoint. That's a "tough gig." I admire their progress and their tenacity.

By necessity, I have done the same. My first husband refuses to talk with me, a fact over which I have no control, so I have chosen to do all I know to do to make amends, look for closure, and release the pain.

During that time, I also entered into a second marriage that I suspect was premature. There were two years in between the divorce and the remarriage, but even though I had stopped reading the romance books, I was still acting out the codependency and compulsive bingeing. Intentional recovery had been put on a shelf, and I had unconsciously defaulted back into dysfunctional thinking and behavior. I also tended to blame my former husband for the failed marriage and not look honestly at my own shortcomings. I looked at some of them and politely overlooked others. You can't change what you don't "see," so I carried baggage into the second marriage. In essence, I was not in the best place to be choosing a new partner, though no one could have successfully shared that with me. As far as I was concerned, I was ready for new love and rushed toward it with hardly a second glance.

In the eighteen months of our courtship, Bill had two episodes of a particular behavior that were very destructive to our relationship. I told him they would need to be addressed, and he said he would do so. I believed him. Our pastor was also aware of the issue and shared his misgivings, but the foundation between Bill and me seemed sufficiently solid, and I decided to extend some "grace" regarding my concerns. We carried out our matrimonial plan, and inevitably, a pattern of good times interrupted by this destructive behavior began to settle into our relationship routine. They were less frequent in the beginning, then increased over the years. I continued to request that we look for help and find ways to change how we handled conflict. But I also knew my own life held imperfections galore, including the compulsive eating, so I carried tons of shame from the addiction and wondered if I deserved what I got. Bill kept saying he was praying about his behavior, and he had accountability partners from time to time, but lasting change did not come.

Meanwhile, from a physical standpoint, my body had become so overloaded with toxins that my kidneys were not functioning properly—the result of thirty years of abuse. I had frequent symptoms of urinary tract infections that couldn't be cleared up with antibiotics, as well as horrible sinus infections from toxins being deposited in those cavities. This was information gathered from my new holistic doctor who had the nutritional and digestive knowledge that I sorely needed.

As for my dad, by February of 2007, he had been suffering for several years with alcoholic dementia and began having a series of mini-strokes. Each one brought greater debilitation, causing his condition to quickly go downhill. He died within three months. My mom and I spent those last few months taking care of him, which actually brought the two of us closer, but the circumstances were nonetheless traumatic. One positive note, however, is that in the last two years of his life, Dad forgot that he liked to drink and, in some ways, became more of the father that I always hoped he would be. It was a bittersweet ending, but as they say in the *Big Book* ... alcoholism is a "cunning, baffling, and powerful"[2] disease.

After the funeral, and much to my surprise, I received a sympathy card from Danny, my sweetheart from high school who I had not seen for twenty-five years. Over time, what began as a situational reconnection ended up turning into an extended friendship. I think we both realized we had not healed from our past severed relationship, as well as the abortion, and there was a need to do so. But it didn't take long for me to become attached to what he offered emotionally. He was very good at verbal affirmations and making me feel special. So, what started out as an effort to heal the past developed into an email relationship that, for me, sometimes crossed the lines of emotional propriety. I never meant for it to go there, but I didn't completely walk away either. The good news is that we did heal the past, but the bad news is that I told my husband that I had allowed myself to be emotionally involved with Danny, and Bill never seemed to really recover. For years, he thought I had done it intentionally.

God's capacity to deal with our humanness, our sin, and our sickness, never ceases to amaze me. His patience is astronomical, as well as His mercy and grace. I was taught that grace is undeserved favor, and looking back, it's easy for me to see His extended hand in so many ways. Mostly ... that I wasn't struck dead by a bolt of lightning on a clear, cloudless day. Some people probably thought I should have been, and some may still pronounce their judgment in that regard. There are times that I, too, don't always know what to do with my life history. But this one thing I do know: I can't change the past. It's already done. So, when the deed is done, and forgiveness is requested, the best recourse at that point is to receive the grace of God.

In recovery, I have also learned the incredible value of accepting the gift of love that God has given. Jesus was the manifestation of that unconditional gift as He paid the price for every time I went astray, missed the mark, blatantly disobeyed, or blindly stumbled into disaster. But it's also true that we can still suffer the consequences set into motion by ungodly or negative choices—a spiritual fact that cannot be denied. That's why God is so invested in directing us toward following His way of living. I don't believe for a second that He takes pleasure in our pain ... even the pain we bring upon ourselves. He wants us free and whole. Simply put, we are so much more pleasant to be around, and so much more useful to God and mankind, when we are free and whole. Why wouldn't He be invested in that process?

What I have found is a God and a Father who deals with my

sin and has compassion for my sickness. Addiction is both sin and sickness, at least in my mind. I don't presume to draw conclusions for anyone else, but my own experience has led to that personal belief.

So, at a time when my actions and decisions were less than stellar, God continued to guide me into avenues of change and growth, and I was gratefully introduced to a healing approach called Caring for the Heart Ministries. Founded by John Regier, the name of this ministry exemplifies the focus as well as the result. I was fifty-two years old, and even though there had been improvement, I was still grappling with woundedness in my soul. The remaining damage needed to be eradicated. Not to where you forget what happened … but to where the emotional effects and lingering residues have been dealt with and washed away. It would take me writing another book to describe the experiences of those years in recovery—of God showing me what had happened to my "heart" and then addressing the wounds in ways that brought wholeness. In that catharsis, I encountered a God who is almost indescribable in His depth of love, caring, and desire to heal. He "blew my socks off" so many times that I lost count. I kept a Healing Journal, and the phrase, "WOW!" shows up on page after page because His heart toward me was so abundantly apparent. I had not met this God before; not that He had changed … but that I had. He was so very faithful, trustworthy, strong, and kind. He was wide open. His heart toward me was wide open. And I had no explanation for it. He looked at my sin, and His heart was wide open. He looked at my sickness, and His heart was wide open. He looked at everything I was … and wasn't … and His heart was wide open. I could feel it. And I was astounded. I spent hours and hours with Him, talking, crying, listening, and receiving. It was fantastic. In essence: this is where I found that Perfect Unconditional Love that I had longed for my entire life.

So, as my second marriage was spiraling downwards, my recovery was spiraling upwards. Both were in process. I don't know how God sees us through all these circumstances and situations, but He does. And He was also helping me learn to trust in, and lean on, other people as well—to create a support system that I had never had. My attendance at an Al-Anon Twelve Step group during that time was a big source of that support and was highly instrumental in helping me understand the true principles of the Twelve Step program. They repeatedly pointed to humility, surrender, and faith in God; and all through the years, even as a Christian, that's where I had been struggling.

... But my "crossroad" was almost at hand.

Fairy Tales:
The Awakening

AT THIS POINT IN TIME, I was still using food to escape from unpleasant emotions, especially stress. The problem was, just about everything stressed me. When Bill and I moved to a larger city in the summer of 2013, I think part of me hoped that the geographical change would somehow lead to a lifestyle change. It did ... I started bingeing more. So, I found an Al-Anon group close by and began attending. Then, one day in December of that year, I made a last-second decision to go to an Alcoholics Anonymous Twelve Step group that was in the same building as the Al-Anon meeting. I'm still not quite sure how that happened, but I'm going to give God the credit. In that first open meeting, as I listened to the drug addicts and alcoholics sharing, I was stunned to realize that I understood every word and identified with almost every experience they were talking about. The revelation exploded deep in my heart: I was an addict. I didn't just eat too much, nor did I just have a food "problem." I was an addict. And the only way out was a total submission to God, choosing to live life His way, not my way. I quietly cried through the whole meeting because, as I accepted that Truth, it felt like five hundred pounds was being lifted off my back. I knew this was the beginning of a new way of life.

... And it has been.

Within four days of that first AA meeting, I stopped the junk food bingeing. I finally, and actually, did Step Three, which was to turn my will and my life over to the care of God. I had a deep realization of two things: God's love for me is real, and trust begins as a choice. So, I made the solid decision that day to trust God one day at a time and took to heart a verse from the first epistle of John that says, "We know how much God loves us, and we have put our trust in his love" (1 John 4:16, NLT). It didn't matter what I had or hadn't done in the past. He loved me then, and He loves me now. I decided to actually believe in that love, receive forgiveness, and totally submit my life to His care.

There's an old cliché that talks about a place where "the rubber meets the road" ... and I was there. After forty years of being addicted to food, bingeing was no longer an option. I had signed up for a crash course in how to live life without eating food compulsively.

Wow.

I became a Twelve Step Meeting Maniac. I went every time I could, which was usually three times a week, and I met quite a few folks who went to a meeting at least once daily. I was soaking up every word that was said because I was hearing that I had to be Honest, Open, and Willing ... the H.O.W. of Twelve Step. From the very first day that I let go of the bingeing, things started changing on the inside of me. I was trying not to get too excited for fear of messing it up, but what I was experiencing was phenomenal. There was new life, solid hope, and this awesome sense of being right in the middle of God's will.

And there was power.

I had times of temptation, but the urges and voices backed off when I declared, often out loud, my total willingness to live life God's way. I meant it. A friend of mine, who is a horseman, once told me that a horse can tell if you really mean what you say when you give a command. If you don't really mean it, they will run you over, so to speak. They won't cooperate. If you do mean it, they submit. They hear it in your voice and feel it in your touch. That thought ran through my head more than once as I was able to overcome the desire to eat compulsively. I mentally, emotionally, spiritually, and verbally took a stance. I meant what I said. And Someone had my back. Being in line with the will of God seemed to plug me into a supernatural strength. And ... I have to admit that something that felt very much like sanity began to dominate my thoughts and emotions. I didn't have a lot of experience with sanity, but when it showed up, I recognized it.

There were many not-so-wonderful times, too. Twelve Step recovery is about facing who and what we are, with the help of God and our support systems, and making right what has been wrong, whenever possible. That's tough stuff. It's about making peace with God, yourself, and others. It's about opening those dark closets that most of us would rather keep locked up, and it's about humility when we share those things with another trusted person. It's about learning to trust, and give, and commune with the human race in ways that work. There are times when the application is very difficult, and sometimes it's excruciating. But the end result is worth it every time. These are things from which you cannot run away—not if you want to get better. Not if you want to live instead of dying.

And live life *well*.

Before hitting bottom, I spent many years trying to avoid emotional pain, and addiction was the ticket that temporarily got me off the hook. But it was never a permanent fix. Never, ever. Each addictive reaction was like a shovel digging the hole a little bit deeper ... the very hole that I was trapped in and trying to exit. If we stay there long enough, we find that the last shovel full of dirt leads only to death.

Even though my kind of addiction takes longer to bring someone to their physical demise, Death is still the name of the train station at the end of the tracks. And there are many signs along the way. It's a long, slow, agonizing ride that touches every part of your being: spirit, soul, and body. I have listened to many addicts and alcoholics who knew that if they "went back out" ... meaning if they used their substance again ... they could easily die that very day. Alcohol poisoning and drug overdoses are killers. In the years that I attended that Twelve Step group, we had more than one person who did just that. They were all tragedies. And their deaths were a very rude wake-up call for the rest of us. The fifth chapter of the *Big Book of Alcoholics Anonymous* says there is no "easier, softer way."[3] So, for a lot of folks it's pretty simple: The Steps work if you work them. If you don't work them ... your money is not refunded ... you just die before your time.

And this brings me to the topic of abstinence.

Obviously, food is not like alcohol or drugs, which can be avoided altogether. With food, the definition of abstinence becomes a more personalized issue. We have to eat in order to survive, so for me, I have focused on why I eat and what I eat. Those are my parameters. I can tell when I'm eating compulsively because it has become so recognizable. I also know that, for myself, high-sugar foods create cravings, so I avoid them for the most part. I also had a severe allergic reaction to the gluten buildup in my system, so I stay away from most gluten products. Thus, my definition of abstinence is: to abstain from using food in compulsive ways and to limit my intake of gluten and high-sugar foods ... one day at a time.

That's what works for me.

Without abstinence, I would have ended up irreparably damaging my liver and kidneys, which would have resulted in my body slowly dying from a long-term overdose of poison. Those organs keep you "cleaned out." And if they become incapable of purification, the toxins build up and begin wreaking havoc systemically. My body was already there. I had become allergic to much of my binge food, and my body reacted as if it were dealing with a poison ... because it was. In small amounts, our bodies are made to break down those substances and expel them in the best possible way. But the body that is subjected to extended, long-term doses of any kind of poison will deteriorate and stop functioning at some point. There are many ways to get there: diabetes, heart disease, high blood pressure, stroke, kidney failure, liver malfunctions, insulin shock, and more.

By the end of my addicted years, I was exhibiting the precursors of type 2 diabetes: low blood sugar episodes with shaking and sweating preceded by blood sugar spikes, weakness and nausea when going too long without food, fatigue, yeast infections, and slow-healing wounds. And I've already mentioned the chronic urinary tract infections, the horrible sinus infections, and what I'm sure was some form of irritable bowel syndrome. It's a proven medical fact that our digestive system is the foundation upon which our overall health is built. When the digestion is compromised, every other bodily system follows suit. It's only a matter of time.

And I was well on my way.

I said all of that just to say: This is a Program of action that saved my life. And since I'm absolutely sure that God led me to Twelve Step, I can say without a doubt that God saved my life. To say that I'm grateful doesn't even begin to touch the depths of what is in my heart.

How do you put a price on a life saved from premature death?

You can't.

And God didn't just save me physically. I also began to experience salvation in the form of mental strength, emotional stability, spiritual vitality, and greater social ease. These are all components of recovery in which I have grown and expanded in my years of addiction-free living. How much would you be willing to pay for all of those benefits? You end up with a life that can actually be enjoyed. That was a new thing for me.

What I really discovered in recovery was how to live life in a way that works—to become a healthy, responsible adult who knows how to deal with emotions, how to set boundaries, how to have happy relationships, and when to do the hard stuff, even when I don't feel like it. I believe it's called growing up. It's embarrassing to say how long it has taken me to get there, but it's definitely a case of "better late than never."

I have listened to many Twelve Step "old-timers" as they shared their experience, strength, and hope ... and suddenly realized that what they were describing was simply maturity. They talked about balancing work and play, about self-regulating, letting go of control, allowing yourself to be imperfect, learning productive ways of handling difficulties, and growing in trust and confidence. And, for me, maturity especially shows up in not being pushed around by emotions. This turned out to be something called "emotional sobriety." The Twelve Step veterans talked about the first measure of sobriety being abstinence—not using your substance of choice. And then they talked about a second sobriety that has to do with what is often the root cause of addiction: out-of-control emotions. You know ... where those emotions eat at you and become vexing and aggravating, creating a negative snowball in your head, and pushing and pressuring you to act unwisely. Been there? Emotional sobriety is a place of peace and balance. It's a place where my feelings are acknowledged, but they don't rule my life. But the ability to live in emotional sobriety comes only from God as I maintain a relationship of dependence on Him, and dependence on my support system as well. If I work the Steps, keep doing what I'm supposed to do, and show up at meetings, He is the one who keeps my thoughts and feelings sane.

Where else are you going to get an education like this for free?

All you have to do is go to a Twelve Step meeting and listen with an open mind and heart.

One of the best rewards of this Program has been the decrease of fear in my life. At first, I had to go through the pain of realizing how much I had actually been controlled and manipulated by fear. Then I had to acknowledge how fear had caused me to make ungodly, hurtful choices in dealing with others. That was a tough one. Then I started learning how to use humility, trust, and faith to step away from fear and find a better way to live life. What a process. And I'm not done. I probably won't be done until I get to heaven. Fear is the big sleeping bear hidden in the back of the cave that roars with a vengeance when poked and prodded. Most of my fear is about self-protection—I have become a master at self-protection—but this "bear" has got to go.

In all fairness, there is a reason why fear has been dominant in my life. A few years ago, through information that I believe God brought to my attention, I realized that I had developed an attachment disorder as a baby because of the circumstances surrounding my birth. It put a name to the emptiness that I had felt all of my life. I learned that when a mother and child don't have the opportunity to bond in a normal, natural way, a deep sense of fear and insecurity is created in the child. It explains why I had a high level of anxiety from day one, why my hair fell out at age three from emotional stress, and why I had such difficulty believing that my mom loved me. It was a huge missing puzzle piece. But God has led me through another leg of my healing journey and worked wonders in my relationship with my mom. We now have a deeper friendship and connection with each other than ever before. It's still a work in progress, but I'll take all the progress I can get. As for the fear and insecurity that was created all those years ago, I know with great certainty that God's restoration will continue until He and I cross the finish line together.

Over time, I have had two major revelations about my "condition." The first one is that I was still dealing with the effects of living in an alcoholic home, as well as the multiple generations of alcoholism. And the second revelation is that I was actually an alcoholic myself— one who had started out abusing alcohol, turned away before the "hook" was completely set, and then transferred my addiction to a different substance. I know now, beyond the shadow of a doubt, that if I was not in recovery and had allowed myself to drink, I would be living in the midst of full-blown alcoholism. That's why my first AA meeting felt so familiar. I have an alcoholic mind. I spent years of my life consuming no alcohol at all. But at one point, I decided a glass of sweet wine wouldn't hurt anything. I was wrong. The craving set in almost immediately, and my thoughts gravitated toward more. It tasted too good. Thankfully, the waving red flags quickly got my attention, and I stopped even the occasional glass. I didn't need any further complications.

As for the effects of an alcoholic home, I thought my season of attending Al-Anon had taken care of that, but I soon realized it had not. What I was actually addressing was a somewhat complicated, hard-to-define malady called "codependency." It's one of those broad-spectrum issues that touches just about every area of one's life. So, I will "throw a wide rope" with this definition: codependency is the development of unhealthy coping patterns in life, primarily, but not always, as a result of living with someone who is or was addicted.[4] Some people with obvious codependency have never lived directly with addiction. However, interestingly enough, there is almost always an addicted relative somewhere in the wings of their family history, such as a grandparent or great-grandparent.

Melody Beattie is a well-known author on codependency, and I learned a great deal through the study of her material, especially

Codependent No More. I will share some highlights that have made a lasting impression over the years: codependent behavior patterns can and do become addictive. I have to work the Twelve Steps for this disease as much as for the food. Codependency can create tendencies such as controlling, caretaking, anxiety, rescuing, and enabling. And it can lead to the more obvious substance addiction. My codependency was manifesting primarily as people-pleasing, wishy-washy boundaries, the need to control, taking on responsibility for other people's problems, and enormous amounts of that fear that I have already mentioned. And, of course ... the other addictions. They all fed into each other, which is usually the case with multiple addictions.[5] So, it certainly makes sense that healing has not been an overnight event.

Recovery seems to come in layers, and God seems to know when I'm ready to look at the next facet of brokenness. Sometimes, I admit that I just get fed up and think, *"Enough, already."* But after a short time, I get back on the treadmill with renewed energy and reach for the next healing goal. The simple fact is that my life is better now than it ever has been, and I don't feel the need to argue with success. It keeps me motivated.

As a result, I have a peace in my soul that I wouldn't trade for anything in this world. I don't have panic attacks anymore, except for a very mild one on the rare occasion. I like and respect who I am, my image of God has changed for the better, and I lost the extra pounds that made me feel fat and ugly. From my greatest weight, that's a total of fifty pounds. I'm comfortable with how I look. I do have a dairy food allergy and a gluten sensitivity, but that just helps me eat in a healthier way. I know that my eating is not perfect, but I don't really expect it to be perfect. I don't know anyone who eats perfectly. On occasion, I may eat too much, and on occasion, I recognize that I've eaten because of an upset—in other words, for emotional reasons. But since December 11, 2013, I have been free one day at a time from the mindless, junk food binges. Food doesn't have power over me like it did in the past.

So, because of those food changes, my liver and kidneys are now functioning normally; I haven't had a sinus infection for years; I no longer have incurable UTIs; and my intestines are doing quite well. Even the supplemental digestive aids that I took for years are no longer needed because my body is now digesting food normally and efficiently. There are many parts of our bodies that will heal themselves if given a chance, and that's exactly what happened to me.

Another change is that I usually don't try to force things to happen anymore—I wait on God, and I let Him run the world. The fear that used to create the need to be in control of people, situations, relationships, and events is simply not there. I'm more relaxed. And happy.

Clearly, everyday living is not without difficulties. I still have shortcomings and character defects to work on and always will. C'est la vie. But the tools are there to use, and I am happy with progress. Life just feels very different.

As for relationships, generally speaking, they are easier. I'm much better at keeping my mouth shut and letting things go. I respond more instead of reacting, which mostly means that I try to stop and think about what I'm going to say or do before I say or do it. That keeps me from a lot of trouble. The changes in my relationships have been from one degree to the next, but the more I heal, the more those interactions evolve into something positive, consistent, and rewarding. All I know is that love heals. When I was able to start truly receiving God's love for me, it changed my ability to love others. Shame and self-hatred create impenetrable walls between people. But acceptance of self and others can form a foundation for relationships built on honesty, openness, and genuine emotional intimacy. What a difference that makes.

Last but not least, I'm so very grateful that I now have what the *Big Book* calls "a faith that actually works." It's a living faith that trusts in a God who loves me and cares about every detail of my life. I have also found wonderful people that I can learn from, trust in, and walk with on this healing journey. They are a huge blessing. God has done such an amazing work, and I totally love Him for it. I don't have one moment of regret when it comes to recovery.

That's an incomplete list, but in my mind, an impressive one. It certainly works for me.

So, maybe you're wondering how the story ends.

Well, I stayed with Bill for seventeen years ... and then I stopped. All trust was gone. Once again returning to my hometown, I got a full-time job, helped my aging mother, enjoyed my kids, and started a new chapter in life. I'm making that sound easy, but divorce is gut-wrenching. I made the choice to move on because it felt necessary. And in the process, I have faced life as an individual instead of having an unhealthy dependence on someone else. To some degree, I realized that I was living with destructive behavior in exchange for financial security. But my security needs to come from God alone, financially and otherwise. I have also learned a powerful lesson about making God my source of true and lasting love. In the past, I mistakenly looked to men to be the perfect love that I so desperately desired.

But I did them a great disservice in placing that responsibility on their heads. I wanted them to fill the bill that only God can fill. No human being can live up to that standard of perfect love. I had to let go of the delusion.

And that's a topic that could fill the pages of another book...

My self-confidence has also had a triple boost due to the fact that I'm in a different living environment, successfully taking on new challenges. I have discovered the ability to handle each one of them with the Lord's help. I can do hard things. I was always afraid I would cut and run because that had been a pattern for me, but I have allowed myself to be different. I have changed. I stayed in the saddle when everything in me wanted to run because I knew I had to. I grew up some more. I have surrounded myself with people who love me as I am, who know how to encourage and affirm. And, as I began to feed my soul with beauty and nature and country, my heart found an undercurrent of peace and joy that flows pretty steadily the majority of the time.

The one constant that always remains is God's love and willingness to keep working in my life—a fact for which I am extremely thankful. Because of His love, I know that recovery is continuing, growth is happening, and progress is being made. I feel closer to God than I ever have.

After returning to my hometown, an old friend came back into my life ... the horseman that I worked with twelve years prior at a therapeutic riding facility. We reconnected, fell in love, and married soon thereafter. He's a Twelve Stepper too. We discovered that we have the same "heart" and now work together to help others in recovery whenever possible. He makes me laugh every single day and loves me about as unconditionally as any human being could. I only hope that I give him as much as he gives me. We have challenges, which is normal, but what a blessing it is to share life with someone who understands where I'm coming from. He wants to grow and expand as a human being as much as I do, and he's willing to "embrace my insanity" when it shows up on occasion, in the same way I choose to "embrace" his. That's a phrase that I read in an interview Emily Platt conducted with Delta Burke and Gerald McRaney. They said they had been married for thirty years because they made a decision long ago to "embrace each other's insanity."[6] What a great way to think about it. It stuck with me.

That's just one example of how I have learned from the experience of others. There is such rich knowledge available if I just listen, and God has brought abundant resources for every leg of this journey, just like He said He would. He has also brought many wonderful people into my life who bring healing, compassion, strength, wisdom, support, and so much more. But equally wonderful, is the knowledge that I have something to give in return. I don't feel empty anymore. I have a love that is much more secure. And from that place of deeper security, I can share my experience, strength, and hope and let God use me to touch the lives of people around me. That's how the healing gets passed on.

There's no fairy tale here. Instead, there's one day at a time with grace and peace, which truly makes life worth living. And that's what I wanted all along.

... A life worth living.

A Bird's-Eye View

SO, WHAT EXACTLY ARE the Twelve Steps?

And how in the world do they work?

Those two questions formed in my mind the first time I sought help for myself in a meeting back in 1988. I had been introduced to the Twelve Steps years before when my dad went to alcoholic rehab, but I have to admit that I paid very little attention to them at that point. It was my *dad* who had the problem, not me, right? But, when the time came that I was wallowing in my own set of despairing circumstances, I decided to give them a second look. Here's what they say.

We:

1. Admitted we were powerless over alcohol (or fill in the blank with whatever addiction you may have) and that our lives had become unmanageable.

2. Came to believe that a Power greater than ourselves could restore us to sanity.

3. Made a decision to turn our will and our lives over to the care of God.

4. Made a searching and fearless moral inventory of ourselves.

5. Admitted to God, to ourselves, and to another human being the exact nature of our wrongs.

6. Were entirely ready to have God remove all these defects of character.

7. Humbly asked Him to remove our shortcomings.

8. Made of list of all persons we had harmed and became willing to make amends to them all.

9. Made direct amends to such people wherever possible, except when to do so would injure them or others.

10. Continued to take personal inventory, and when we were wrong, promptly admitted it.

11. Sought through prayer and meditation to improve our conscious contact with God, praying only for knowledge of His will for us and the power to carry that out.

12. Having had a spiritual awakening as the result of these Steps, we tried to carry this message to alcoholics (or those still suffering) and to practice these principles in all our affairs.[7]

When I first read those Steps, I couldn't make much sense out of them. I had a partial understanding, but it was almost like reading a secret code that was going to have to be deciphered to get the full message. For the life of me, I didn't initially see how these Twelve Steps had the power to change lives, but from what I knew about Alcoholics Anonymous, that's *exactly* what they could do. It wasn't until I went to my first AA meeting, and began to listen to people share their stories, that comprehension began to unfold. Some people say that the Twelve Step program isn't something you understand with your mind. It's something you "catch." I will readily say that there is a supernatural element that permeates this Program. When you show up with an open heart, God gets involved. What I observed right away, because of my Christian background, was that the *principles* of the Steps were Biblical. So, even though I didn't have an instant understanding, I had a certain amount of faith that they at least *could* work. I figured if anyone had the wisdom and ability to fix something, surely it was God. He's a pretty smart Guy, right?

So, as I took a closer look at the Steps, and listened carefully to the words of others in recovery, the elements of the Program started floating to the surface. I saw a healthy dependence, solid faith, a complete surrender to God, self-examination, confession, character change, humility, forgiveness, repentance, making amends for wrongdoing, accountability, daily assessments, staying in a growing relationship with God, and paying it forward through purposeful living and sharing the message. I knew those were all positive, godly things. Actually, they sounded like the components of true discipleship.

But this was no small order.

It was going to take guts to go down this road. And I was glad the journey didn't require me to fly solo. It was also a relief to see that I didn't have to reinvent the wheel all by myself; there was absolutely no need. My previous, dysfunctional tendency was to try to do everything on my own, which only created hardship and anguish. But with the Twelve Steps, I could see that the tools were in place, the support was there, and all I had to do was jump in and take one step forward.

So, I did.

Now that I have some recovery under my belt, I find myself looking back over the months and years, feeling a little amazed at the wisdom that is so freely given, the strength that comes as a natural result of working this Program, and the way God uses other people to speak into my life. The blessings are beyond description. I'm convinced that the simplicity of the Steps is no accident, but rather, the inspired design of the Holy Spirit. They are Steps of action that show me how to live life successfully. That doesn't mean that my days are without challenges, difficulties, or hardships; it *does* mean that God shows me how to handle those things in ways that work. I lived for most of my adult life in a place of fear, depression, addiction, and self-hatred, so, learning to live with peace and contentment means a lot to me. That's why I'm willing to follow through with the three requirements for this Program: 1) rigorous honesty, 2) an open mind, and 3) the willingness to participate wholeheartedly.

I'm not sure if everyone learns the same way I do, but it's hard for me to walk into a new job, or a new project, and have people start throwing a lot of details at me without explaining the vision. I need to see at least the outline of how it all goes together. I need a birds-eye view. When you get a glimpse of the big picture, the breakdown of the details becomes much easier to understand. So, here's my overview of the Twelve Steps:

I once heard a pastor talking about being ready ... ready for change ... and that's exactly the place that I came to in my life. I was not only incredibly tired of the miserable way I was living, but I was also tired enough to actually seek change. But I had finally realized that I could not do this in my own strength. Being powerless to change was very humbling, but very good, because that's Step One. Acknowledging my powerlessness leads to humility, and humility is designed to lead me to a place of rest because it teaches me to truly depend on God and others. But how do I depend on God? I never got that "dependence thing" quite right in the past.

My belief in God began when I was very young, and I asked Jesus into my heart at the age of twenty, but in the Twelve Step program, what I came to understand was that I did not have a *fully-functioning faith*. Life had "muddied the view," so to speak. So, as I was working Step Two, I came to believe in two things: 1) that God actually loved me, and 2) that He *wanted* to restore me to sanity and had the power to do so. For me, sanity is being able to think right, believe right, and choose right, all of which lead to acting right. I came to believe partly because I made the choice to believe, and partly because in AA meetings I heard people sharing how God had restored *them*. It only made sense that He would also do it for me. I call this contagious faith. And it works.

At that point, I had come to the end of *my* power, I had come to believe that God *did* have the power, so then it became a question of how do I *receive* the power? What I learned is that the power is directly connected to a total surrender, specifically of my will and my life. I realized that as long as I was habitually doing what God didn't want me to do; I was not surrendering my will. But the revelation came: surrendering my will GAVE me the power to make right choices. Surrender *is* the power connection. This is a one-time event, but it's also a daily and even minute-to-minute choice. And that's Step Three.

It is, admittedly, a big change from the way I used to live. I operated in fear and self-centeredness much of the time. And I had a tendency to want to eat what I wanted to eat, control what I wanted to control, and feel what I wanted to feel. But when I hit bottom, I wanted *change* more than I wanted to stay stuck in my old ways, so I made the decision to trust God and to truly respect Him. Surrendering to God's rule and authority is an act of respect and a reasonable service, which is pointed out in Romans 12:1. After all, He is God, and I am not. When I gave myself to God, withholding nothing, dramatic change started happening, at least from my point of view.

The first three Steps help me get to a different and better place with *God*.

The next four Steps are about dealing with *me*.

I hated myself; I was filled with shame; I felt inadequate; I blamed myself for almost everything; and I didn't think I was worthy to take up space on the planet. I had secrets; I lived a double life; I wore a "mask" in public; and the last thing I wanted to do was take a good look at my inner world. It was dark and scary in there. But many years ago, one-on-one counseling helped me begin that process, as well as working with Caring for the Heart Ministries in more recent years. I have since learned that it's not as scary as it seems. Step Four is about getting honest with myself about who I am, what I've done, the choices I've made, and the character I have. What enables me to reach this level of honesty is the knowledge that God can and will *change* that which is revealed. Otherwise, I would be completely intimidated and overcome by hopelessness.

It has been said that we're only as sick as our secrets. The point is: what I try to hide from myself and others makes me sick inside. And when I'm sick inside, I want to act out my addictions. Step Four is where I begin to learn personal responsibility and start moving toward greater emotional maturity. And it's about stopping the blame game and no longer wishing that everyone *around* me would change. I can't change anyone else, but with God's help, I can work on *me*. This Step should also include the acknowledgment of what is good and positive. No one is "all bad," and it's good to pursue some balance.

So, then I take my discoveries of what is inside of me and share them out loud. I don't have to tell the whole world all my dark secrets, but I DO need to tell God, myself, and one other trustworthy person. That's Step Five. It can bring freedom from guilt and shame, and provide a new perspective. And, in the telling, we can create a clean slate and a fresh beginning. Step Five has power to heal.

The next project is figuring out *what to do* with the things that I have learned about myself. There are flaws and shortcomings that I don't want to keep, so Step Six tells me that I need to get ready to let them go. I have learned that I sometimes want to hang on to certain character defects such as fear, anger, self-pity, or a judgmental attitude. I've had really good *uses* for those things, like creating distance between me and others and keeping myself "emotionally safe." For a short time, I wasn't sure I wanted to let them go. But I have realized that they also keep me in a self-focused prison that generates unhappiness, depression, immaturity, and stunted personal growth.

Then, once I'm ready, I begin to ask God to remove the negative stuff that I have used for many years to cope with life. He has shown me that I can make different choices, implement healthier ways to cope, and actually feel good about myself in the process! This is Step Seven, which I take from a position of humility, depending on God to make these inner changes as I add my agreement and cooperation. I do this in faith. The truth is, I was aware of many of these character defects long before I got involved with the Program, and when I tried in my own strength to get rid of them, I couldn't. But when I started turning them over to God, I found that He could work the miracles that were needed. A few defects have disappeared overnight, and others have changed more slowly, but the end result is still the same: I'm a different person and a better person—someone I actually like.

The next two Steps have to do with my relationships with others.

It didn't take me long to figure out that I had lots of relationship problems that were generating emotional pain and sometimes even torment. Steps Eight and Nine teach me to stop running away, and to take responsibility for *my* part, which often brings resolution and an end to conflict. So, I made a list of people that I had harmed and started tackling the work of asking for forgiveness and making amends—always with the help of God. This wasn't about what other people had done *to* me; this was about *my* behavior toward others. I actually began this process in 1976, the year after I became a Christian, so it wasn't completely new and foreign. But, as I went forward this time, I also prayed for God to create opportunities for me to accomplish the task. I asked Him to supernaturally set up the "meetings" with others in the most natural ways possible with both parties prepared to make peace. The Lord has been very faithful in this process, and almost all of my amends have been received well and even reciprocated.

Like the other Steps, the principles held in these two have the power to clean out the "poisons" in our lives, the only exception being: if my amends would actually cause harm to someone. In those instances, God shows me an alternate path that accomplishes the same goal. My experience is that God guides very effectively in these endeavors because of His vested interest in the wholeness of everyone involved.

After all this effort and hard work, Step Ten helps me *maintain* healthy relationships with myself and others, as I keep daily tabs on my actions, words, attitudes, and choices. When I mess up, I apologize. And I also use this Step to monitor my emotions and to assess who or what is in control of my life. Is it God? Is it someone else? Or is it my feelings? I'm learning that fine balance between acknowledging my feelings and not letting them rule my life. When I fall short in any of these areas, I take it to God and make changes right away. If I don't take care of it, I'm once again setting myself up for addictive behavior and creating space for continued pain. Frankly, I've had enough pain of my own making. I'd rather have sobriety. In the *Big Book of Alcoholics Anonymous* it says we have "a daily reprieve contingent on the maintenance of our spiritual condition."[8] Step Ten is key to that maintenance.

The last two Steps are about growing with God and passing it on.

How can I expect to have a peaceful life, significant joy, and overcoming power if I'm not close to the Source of all those things? Step Eleven is about continuing to develop my relationship with God and staying "plugged in." It's also about keeping it simple: I pray for God's will to be done and the power to carry that out. I can personally get myself into a lot of trouble being analytical, and it only takes me half of a minute to overanalyze myself right into a corner. This Step reminds me that it's important to stay focused and consistent; simple goals can facilitate the process. Now, in every situation, I can ask God two things: 1) What is Your will? and 2) Please give me the power to do what You want me to do. Amen.

The last Step is one of the most important ways I have of keeping my freedom—I give it away. I intentionally share my experience, strength and hope in many different ways; and every time I do, I reinforce the principles that have led me to a new way of living. This is how I practice getting it right. And I really want to get this right.

These Twelve Steps are steps of ACTION ... they require me to "get out of the boat." I don't just do them once and call it done. I use them every day to live my life. I see them as Biblical concepts that actually exemplify the life of a disciple of Jesus. When I read the Gospels, I find Him teaching these principles at every turn, and that's because they work ... if you work them.

I want to be a disciple of Jesus.

I want a life that works.

How about you?

Step One:
Failure or Faith

I REMEMBER HAVING A POSTER in my music room many years ago that showed a photograph of a beautiful sunset. Below it, the caption said in so many words that God did exist, and His title had not been conferred upon *me*. I thought that was a great poster, but in all honesty, I didn't get it. I had two particular problems: One was that, in spite of the fact that I believed God was great and powerful, I wasn't sure how to trust Him. The second had to do with the fact that some part of me thought that I should be able to keep my life manageable without help from anyone else. It was an embarrassment to think that I couldn't. So, I don't know if I was persistent, stubborn, or stupid, but, for almost forty years, I kept trying to live a manageable life in my own power ... before I finally gave up.

Step One says: *We admitted we were powerless over (fill in the blank with your addiction)—that our lives had become unmanageable.*[9]

As for me, I was powerless over my food addiction and my codependency.

It was pretty humiliating for me to realize that I was making choices that I couldn't stop making. For a long time, I just thought the bingeing was "a problem" or a "bad habit." I knew beyond a shadow of a doubt that it was not a good thing, but I was absolutely convinced that if I would just exercise enough will power, or make a solemn promise to God, or confess enough times that I was victorious in Christ; then I would stop eating the excess food and be done with it. But that never happened, and I was ashamed to admit that no matter how hard I tried, the needed willpower was just not manifesting. When I was a full-time homemaker, I often thought if I had a job outside of the home, and wasn't alone so much, then there wouldn't be a problem at all. If I just stayed busy, then I wouldn't have the time or the desire to overeat. In other words, there was always some element outside of myself that would make it all better. It was the "dangling carrot." At other times, my mental processes, my emotions, and my active choices were so distorted and confused that I really thought someone should just "put me away." And there were times I would have been thankful if someone had. Compulsive bingeing made me feel crazy. As a matter of fact ... it *was* crazy.

Case in point: I once pulled the remainders of a bakery cake out of our alley trash can in order to finish what I hadn't eaten during my binge from the day before. I always tried to hide the fact that I was bingeing, so if there were any "leftovers," I would dispose of them secretly. The outside trash can was usually a safe place because, normally, no one was going to have a reason to rummage around in a plastic trash bag already taken out for pickup. That is, unless you're addicted to food, and you decide that you want to finish off the uneaten half of the layer cake that's inside. Well, my cake was still in its cardboard and cellophane bakery box, so I fished it out of the bag of smelly garbage that had been sitting in our metal can for twenty-four hours. The poor thing was partially smashed from its secret disposal, but once it hit my taste buds, what was the difference? I ate the rest of it. I was twenty-five years old when that incident happened, and was, by then, well entrenched in my sickness. But it took me thirty-five more years to come to the end of myself.

No one knows, exactly, what it takes to hit bottom. If I could come up with a standard formula, I'd be a billionaire. The fact is: it's different for every person. But I have learned a couple of things. The first one is this: Coming to the end of myself was the best thing that ever happened to me next to Jesus. Secondly, if someone hasn't hit bottom yet, they can pray for it. I am amazed at the things I can ask God to do for me, when before it never occurred to me to ask at all!

Step One is about giving up ... in the best possible sense of the word. It usually sounds something like: "This has got to change. I can't stand living like this for one more second. BUT - I - CAN'T - CHANGE - IT." I can't figure it out. I can't read enough information, work through enough self-help books, talk to enough people, confess enough scripture, or make enough promises. I can't stop
... in my own strength.

When I finally arrived at Step One, in some ways it felt like failure, for the simple fact that I couldn't accomplish the goal on my own. Not for one second did I like admitting that I needed help. That was paramount to admitting weakness or saying that something was actually wrong with me. After all those years of trying to look perfect, admitting that I wasn't perfect was like trying to swallow a golf ball. And, if I needed help, that meant I was going to have to depend on someone else, and I didn't know how to do that. I didn't want to do that. I felt like I couldn't depend on people when I was growing up, so what was going to make it any different or any better now? Besides, I really didn't want anyone else in the driver's seat; that had been my private space for a very long time.

Walls of Resistance.

... But there's something about hitting bottom that melts down resistance like butter in a hot skillet. Pride and fear take a back seat. When you're drowning, and you don't want to drown, does it really matter who throws the life saver? Does it matter that you can't swim as well as you thought you could? Does it matter that you can't save yourself? In the face of death, that all becomes a moot point. Your focus changes; you just want to be saved.

Period.

There's a reason why the Coast Guard trains their rescue swimmers to jump into the ocean and come alongside a victim in peril. Of course, the Coast Guard member is there to provide physical assistance, but for the victim, there's also something very reassuring about not being alone when you think you're going to die. And when that someone has the resources to save you, it's even more reassuring.

Resistance, however, is our gut response to fear. When my addiction was completely out of control and I couldn't stop, I was quietly terrified. I felt like I was suffocating, so I struggled all the more to remove the weight that was holding me down. But the fact remains: If you're drowning, the trained rescuer ordinarily maneuvers you into a position of nonresistance, where your thrashing arms and legs are powerless to cause harm. They encourage you to relax, breathe, and rest from your efforts. The message is: stop resisting the fact that you need help. When you tense up, get rigid, and continue fighting... you sink. You go under. You die.

So, stop resisting.

I can't tell you how many times I tried, and failed, to resist the temptation to binge in my own strength. It surpassed the point of ridiculousness many, many years ago. But there's a reason why the second Step addresses the topic of insanity. Insanity is a word that may create a level of discomfort in some people, but it aptly describes my state of mind before, during, and after a multitude of failed attempts that ended in nothing but frustration. So, a day came when I had to look my insanity in the eye and get comfortable with it. I looked at the unmanageability of my life and took off the blinders, the rose-colored glasses, and the cloak of denial.

Okay. Insanity is there. Unmanageability is there.

And I'm supposed to be okay with that?

Essentially ... yes.

Admitting you are powerless may feel very strange; it feels like you're doing the opposite of what you should do. There's a familiar verse that talks about God's ways being higher than the ways of man (Isaiah 55:8–9, NLT), and this couldn't be truer than with Step One. But when you finally admit that you're powerless, it opens your mind and heart to new possibilities. It's like closing one door and turning around to open another. The day that I gave up, was the day things started to turn around. I got comfortable saying to myself: I can't change this, but God can. When I'm powerless, God isn't. When I run out of strength, God is just getting started. That's when I began walking in the power that only He can give, and what initially felt like failure turned into this wonderful thing called faith.

That was for the bingeing. But what about the codependency?

With the bingeing, I had to admit that I didn't have the power within myself to change ME. With the codependency, I had to admit that I had no power to change anyone ELSE. I spent my whole life trying to control other people, so they wouldn't hurt me, which definitely made my life unmanageable. I was spinning my wheels all the time. I had no idea that I was trying to control anyone. I was simply trying to keep myself safe, and that wasn't necessarily a conscious thought. It was just how I lived my life. I was afraid of disapproval. I was afraid of rejection. I was afraid of correction. I was afraid of shame. I was afraid of criticism. I was afraid of being judged and misjudged. I was afraid of making mistakes. I was afraid of being inadequate. I was afraid of people. And I was afraid of myself. Every day was a battle with fear. And every day, on some level, I tried to control the world around me, so I wouldn't feel any pain. Needless to say, it didn't work. But boy did I try. I tried really hard. It was exhausting.

Without realizing it, I had also learned the "art" of manipulation. But I didn't call it manipulation; I called it "having influence." I was only trying to "influence" someone to make a certain choice or do a certain thing. That wasn't so bad, was it? To be honest, every aspect of my codependency seemed to circle back to the issue of control. I wanted to be in control because I was afraid. I wanted to be in control because I didn't trust anyone else to be watching out for my good. I wanted to be in control because so many circumstances in my life had been out of my control, and I ended up devastated and suffering with emotional pain. It certainly made sense to me that I needed to keep everything and everyone in their "rightful" place ... where I wanted and needed them to be. When I felt something getting out of control, anxiety would start growing in the pit of my stomach, spreading through my body like a fast-moving virus. If it went on long enough, panic began to take over and paralyze my thoughts. I would go into a "brain freeze." It was, at times, completely overwhelming. So, I was highly motivated to make sure that nothing got out of control. I learned to be very vigilant.

In 1985, when we lived in Maryland, my mother-in-law and sister-in-law were scheduled to fly in and visit over Thanksgiving. They lived fifteen-hundred miles away, so this was not a frequent event. I was bound and determined to have the house and the yard looking absolutely perfect, which was my normal mode of operation when we had company. I didn't realize it at the time, but I was still operating under the false pretense that perfection bought acceptance. And I was afraid of rejection, especially from my in-laws. My twisted logic told me that if everything looked perfect, they would have no reason to judge me unfavorably.

For three days before they arrived, I cleaned every inch of our home and continued my efforts outside in our very large yard. The leaves had not yet been picked up that fall, so I made it my job to make our property look like a photo from a *House and Garden* magazine. On the third day, there was a cold wind and a misty rain trying to sabotage my labors, but I persevered. By the time our company arrived, I was completely exhausted. And when they left three days later, I came down with a virus. It started with a terrible sore throat and high fever that quickly moved into my lungs. In a short time, I had pneumonia and ended up in the emergency clinic, dehydrated and in need of a heavy dose of antibiotics. I had literally made myself sick trying to be perfect in order to avoid rejection, when the truth is: I have no control over what other people think. And it's as simple as that. When did I become so afraid of what other people think about me? I don't know. But honestly, I don't remember a time in those years when I wasn't afraid of that very thing.

Part of my healing, now, is to do the best I can and leave the rest with God. Step One is largely about me finally realizing that being in control is like a mirage off in the distance ... I never quite reach my destination. There is very, very little that I actually have control over—certain things, yes, but not much. In my past, however, that didn't keep me from trying! For instance, when my kids were young, I kept no sugar in the house. I was a compulsive binger who binged on different forms of sugar, salt, and fat. I couldn't keep sugar in the house; I would eat it until it was gone, whatever it was—ice cream, cookies, cake, donuts, candy, you name it. Since I was afraid my children would follow in my footsteps, I decided to remove all temptation, thinking I was being a responsible mom. Years later, my daughter shared with me that, in order to have something sweet, she would go to church and steal extra cookies from the children's department. They always had snack-time treats, and the usual limit was two cookies per child, but here was my daughter sneaking multiple goodies into her pockets when no one was watching. Her response to my efforts to control her sugar consumption was, in effect, typical. But it took me a very long time to wake up to reality.

In regard to codependency ... I had a plethora of Step One lessons to learn. And drawing again from my study of *Codependent No More*, here are some of the gold nuggets gathered and applied from those pages: I had to acknowledge that all my efforts to change or control others were not working. I was powerless. I couldn't change anybody. I needed to admit that trying to do so made my life unmanageable. The only person I can change is me. I can change my thoughts, my reactions, my attitudes, my choices, my victim mentality, and my viewpoint. I can detach, whether it's detaching from another person's choices, or sometimes from the person themselves. I'm not responsible for other people or their choices or their thoughts or their feelings. I have learned that they are responsible for those things. I am responsible for my choices, my thoughts, and my feelings. No more blame game. No more "poor me." No more being a "victim." No more "if only you hadn't ..." No more trying to "save" someone else, "fix" someone else, or "care" for someone else in ways that they are capable of doing themselves.[10]

My job is to love people and help people only in the ways that God instructs me to love and help. Sometimes I get confused about that, but more clarity comes with every new situation. And now that I have stopped trying to run the world and everybody in it, I'm amazed at how much more time I have!

What I finally concluded was that, in order to admit my powerlessness and let go of control, I had to come back to the same basic issue that I had stumbled over for decades. Can I, or will I, trust God? Step One brought me to a crystal-clear fork in the road in that regard, and I had to reset my spiritual compass. I had to stand in front of God inside my heart and make a choice. One of the foundational components of Twelve Step is something called willingness, and I became willing to make the choice to trust. I can't tell you exactly how that happened, but I can tell you that when you start working the Twelve

Step program, you can expect to see miracles in your life. They may be big, or they may be small, but I have experienced too many amazing things to ever assume they were spawned by something ordinary. How do I explain that one moment I lacked willingness, and the next moment I had it? That one moment I couldn't make the choice to trust, and the next moment I could? Accepting my powerlessness, and becoming willing to move toward change, was like plugging into a live wall socket where the divine power of God finally made contact with my heart, my soul, my mind, my will, and my emotions. Game on! I'm aware that it doesn't happen exactly that way for everyone, but that's how it happened for me. And I have discovered that there is One who has more power and more wisdom than I, and He loves me enough to share it. I can trust Him.

I have also discovered that God can, and will, put other trust-worthy people in my life who have wisdom and experience to share—wisdom and experience that I need. In the past, I naively gave people too much power to hurt me, and as a result, I became as reluctant to trust other people as I was to trust God. But with the parting of the curtain, God has revealed to my mind and heart that recovery is a journey to be taken in the company of fellow sufferers because He predestined and ordained us to walk in community. We help each other to heal; His creative design declares it to be so. The simple fact is: we need each other. I'm convinced that the only circumstance in which God would allow me to be set free totally on my own, with just me and God, is if I were stranded on a desert island, with no other human being in sight and no hope of rescue.

I have to admit that I wasn't very excited about this community aspect of recovery. Since I can't control what other people do, that makes life unpredictable and "messes" with my desire to protect myself from emotional pain. So, I had to come to a place where I was willing to admit that I'm also powerless over that very thing—meaning, I can't keep emotional pain from happening. But in that powerlessness, I have uncovered a new and precious covenant with God: When I trust God with my life, my relationships, and my feelings, He absolutely obligates Himself to protect me, keep me, heal me, and deliver me. That doesn't mean I'm pain-free; it simply means that I'm never alone in that pain, and God's covenant promise is to see me through to the other side and *bring good in the process*.

With food addiction, as well as codependency, I am extremely grateful for the day that I accepted my powerlessness. That acceptance was a healthy choice and a godly choice, and it has led to a much better, and often miraculous, way of life. It began with enough humility to finally let go. One of my favorite Twelve Step mottos says: Let Go and Let God.[11] I did not have the strength to overcome my addictions, but God did. It was an admission of defeat, closely followed by a new hope. I could see that there was a way out, but it wasn't going to be easy. It felt like jumping off a cliff, trusting that God's arms were waiting there to catch me. And when you're trapped on a cliff ledge, which is where I stood in my addictions, there's just no other way to go forward ... but to jump.

Step Two:
Finding True North

OUT OF ALL THE TWELVE STEPS, I have to say
that Step Two is my sentimental favorite. When I finally came to
the realization that my life was clearly out of control, it wasn't hard
for me to swallow the fact that my actions and behaviors had gone
beyond the realm of what most people consider normal. I had held
suspicions in that regard for many, many years. I also knew that those
actions and behaviors left me feeling ashamed, humiliated, demor-
alized, and often appalled. I occasionally had an experience where it
felt like I was outside of my body, watching myself make choices that
were in complete opposition to the desires of my true heart. So, it
was somewhat of a relief to read in the second Step that, yes indeed,
I was crazy. Otherwise, God would not need to restore me to sanity.
At least my thinking was relatively clear in *that* respect. Apparently,

all addicts frequently depart from sanity, but in many or most cases, we are blissfully unaware. It has become "normal."

Step Two says: *Came to believe that a power greater than ourselves could restore us to sanity.* [12]

Merriam Webster defines sanity as "soundness of mind,"[13] and in my case, since I'm not sure I was *ever* sane, putting my faith in this step was maybe the beginning of sanity, rather than the restoration. And that's okay. If that's what God needed to do, He was perfectly capable. But insanity was something I could describe to anyone who cared to ask. When you want to stop eating, and you can't, it feels crazy. When you hate yourself and can't seem to change, it feels like a looney bin. When you try to squeeze healthy love out of someone who doesn't have healthy love to give, that will drive you nuts. When you keep making the same choices that haven't worked in the past, hoping that somehow it will be different this time, you have crossed over into an alternate reality.

The problem with addiction is that you don't see true reality in front of you. Situations, people, relationships, yourself, and circumstances are all seen through distorted filters and a wall of denial. Some of my distorted filters were created by my own reactions to life, and some came from growing up in an alcoholic home where things got a little twisted trying to revolve around someone else's addiction. That's where codependency (which we will discuss en route) can gain a foothold. When a healthy model of sanity doesn't exist in your immediate surroundings, insanity becomes normal. And that's what happened to me. Just to clarify, when I use the word "insanity," I'm not talking about being stark raving mad and completely out of touch with the real world. My personal definition of insanity is: *continuing* in a way of thinking, believing, behaving, and living … that doesn't work. I never learned how to think healthy thoughts, deal with my emotions in a healthy way, or respond to life with healthy choices. I was a negative, emotionally immature, impulsive, fearful *reactor*. In most situations, I didn't know how to assess and respond with any semblance of wisdom or operate with personal boundaries. I just had off-the-wall, knee-jerk reactions to everything and everybody. Or I would freeze up in a state of fear. Or I would turn to food and eat. Or all the above. I did not approach life with mental/emotional soundness. In all honesty, my growing up years were a combination of childhood immaturity mixed with dysfunction, but chronological age did not bring a cure.

Whether it was from physiological or environmental causes, my "head" just wasn't typical.

I didn't have the standard model.

The *Big Book of Alcoholics Anonymous* is full of stories about people living with a mental state called the "alcoholic mind." And they clearly write that this state of mind has no real defense against the desire to drink. It's a form of insanity where there seems to be no human resistance to the thought of using the addictive substance or acting out the addictive behavior; in fact, you can move into the addictive action without even thinking about it.

I have experienced this. I was doing fine with my eating one day, with no thought of bingeing … until I had some Christmas casserole for supper. It had cheese and other dairy products in it, which is something I don't usually eat, so eating small portions had been a pleasurable treat. But that night as I ate the casserole, all of the sudden I wanted to eat everything in sight. And I did. There was no resistance, no second thought—just acquiescence. I moved from normal eating to bingeing in a split second and felt completely powerless to make a different choice. Every addict knows what this mind is about after the compulsion stops, but I don't think we know much about it when we're still acting out our addictions. It's part of the insanity. There were many, many years that I simply lived with it, not really analyzing how my mind was working or where it was going. And even when I *did* start analyzing my thoughts and behaviors, I still couldn't stop.

I have an alcoholic mind.

And the truth remains: knowledge does not cure. My belief, in concurrence with many others, is that the supernatural power of God is the only answer to this dilemma. I didn't have one bit of natural power to come against the urge to binge that night—just an instantaneous reaction. And it became a stark reminder that I have a disease. When it comes to food, my mind just doesn't operate like a normal person. In past moments when I wanted to binge, my thinking probably didn't make sense to anyone but me. Then after I acted out compulsively, I would suddenly "wake up" and shake my head in disbelief. How did that just happen?

Yes, it's "cunning, baffling, and powerful."

But instead of alcohol addiction ... it's food addiction.

So, then I came face-to-face with the insurmountable problem: the food is out of control, my mind is goofy, and I'm powerless. Now what do I do? The Twelve Steps tell me that the *only thing I can do is choose to believe that a Power greater than myself can restore me to sanity.* When you have an incurable disease ... you need a miracle. And in this case, it's a one-day-at-a-time miracle that leads to normal eating and freedom from the compulsion.

But when I came to Twelve Step, the whole *Faith and Miracle* business had eluded my grasp thus far. I needed a jump-start.

For me, and maybe for a lot of people, Step Two was like being handed a compass after being lost in a dense forest for many years. I needed to locate "true north" in order to navigate out of the woods. I had traveled through life depending mostly on my own knowledge, my own intellect, and my own ability, which is how I got lost in the first place. Somehow, I had the idea that God created me, stuck me on the planet, and left me there to stumble through life alone—a belief apparently carried over from abandonment, or the attachment disorder, or decades of emotional pain. Or who knows what.

But Step Two says that God has the power to make my mind and my life sane again. What a statement! That clearly indicates that there is a God who is highly interested in being personally involved with me and has the power to make a phenomenal difference. Who is this God?? I had to conclude that maybe I had not fully come to know this Person, even though I had been a Bible-reading, praying, churchgoing Christian for thirty-eight years before I began to follow the Twelve Step program. I could see that my underlying beliefs about God, and how I thought He operated in my life, were going to have to change. I believed that God would do things for *other* people but not for me. I didn't think I deserved any help. And I sure didn't deserve an outright miracle.

On occasion, I would see a glimpse of a different God who truly offered unconditional love with no prerequisites, but the image would slip through my fingers like water disappearing into dry, thirsty sand. I was not *connecting* with the all-powerful God of the universe. I was not *submitting* the totality of my life to Jesus, the Lord of All. I was not *entrusting* my being to the care of the Good Father. I was still living life on my own. I was living life MY way because that was my "comfortable groove." I listened to Christian music, wore my cross necklace, and carried my Bible to church; but I was, virtually, still lost in the woods.

I also lived in a land called Never Enough. I was never enough. I was always falling short. And I thought God was standing over my shoulder shaking His head in disappointment. I didn't truly know Him. And it's hard to trust someone you don't know. So, even though I had spent years praying, studying the Word, teaching the Word, and confessing the Word, I finally realized that I didn't *believe* much of the Word. I had very little genuine faith. And now, here I was, at the end of myself and my own strength, having to accept the fact that without help, I was sunk. *Faith* was about as familiar to me as admitting I was powerless. But where else do you go in light of the predicament faced by all of us who are addicted? When you finally accept the fact that you need help, you are essentially "forced" to believe that help is available. But if it works ... who cares how it arrives? I have come to understand very clearly that a viable relationship with God, based on *believing*, was the missing component in my life.

So, how does all of this faith and believing tie into the Twelve Step program?

As I did a little research, I discovered that the Twelve Steps were inspired, in part, by a Christian organization founded in the 1920s called The Oxford Group. This was actually a movement which purposed to lead individuals into a living, breathing, life-changing relationship with Jesus Christ as true disciples. And in order to be true disciples, they purposed to follow certain Biblical principles and guidelines on a daily basis. The founders of Alcoholics Anonymous were initially involved with the Oxford Group and carried over certain tenets such as surrendering your life to God (a higher power) and asking for daily guidance from that power. So, the God factor in the Twelve Steps was a primary component from the beginning. The belief was, and is, that God (a higher power) is central to any true recovery.[14]

I had believed that in my head, but did I believe it in my heart?

I can vividly remember the first time I found my way into an Alcoholics Anonymous meeting. On more than one occasion, I had glanced into the AA room as I started up to the second floor where an Al-Anon group met simultaneously in the same meeting hall. But that morning, something compelled me to turn and walk into the AA room instead. I was alone, didn't know a soul, and initially felt awkward and out of place. But as the alcoholics around me began to share their stories one by one, my heart began to melt. Every prideful wall that I had ever erected in order to "preserve my dignity" came crashing down like the walls of Jericho because these people were telling my story. They were sharing the heartache and pain from *my* life, even though I was a total stranger to all of them. Sitting there with tears rolling down my cheeks, I could feel God reaching into my heart and embracing me with something that felt like *Hope*. It took me a moment to recognize it, because it had been so long since my soul had been touched by anything akin to hope. It felt wonderful. It surrounded me like a gentle breeze floating off a misty lake at sunrise. Amazingly, there it was. And all I could do was cry. That morning, something changed on the inside of me. If I were to try to put it into words, I would have to say that … my heart began to believe.

Step Two is written with the phrase "came to believe," and that's exactly what it means. For some people, it can happen all at once, but for many others, it happens over a period of time. I knew that the commitment I made to God in 1975 had been genuine, even though my life seemed solitary and largely powerless. But as I sat in that first AA meeting, a thought kept rolling around in my head over and over again: if God is willing to help these alcoholics whose lives have been so very similar to mine, maybe He is actually willing to help me too.

In the days following, several questions began to percolate.

I could hear God's voice asking me, "Will you choose to believe? Will you choose to believe that I really do love you? Will you choose to believe that My power is there to heal and restore YOU?"

I realized that I could stay stuck in my doubt, fear, and unbelief, or I could make the choice to try something different. I could be *willing* to believe. And that's what I chose to do. Since my previous way of living life was not working at all, the choice to try something different was actually very logical, sensible, and wise.

Why hadn't I thought of this before???

I don't know. But I'm just happy to say that I finally got there.

I'm not sure why God used the Twelve Step program to help me come to this place, but He did. As I sat in those first few meetings, the faith and trust exemplified in others started to rub off on me. And now, every time I go to a meeting and hear how God is showing up in people's lives, faith and trust rub off on me all over again. I have come to believe in this loving, powerful God by believing in the God that Jesus talks about in the Gospels *and* by listening to the stories of others who have gone before me in Twelve Step. The faith I hear *in others* becomes contagious.

... And I have come to recognize this as a gift from the Father.

In the beginning of my recovery, the tendency to fall back into old ways was ever present. That's why it was so important to keep coming back to meetings for the positive reinforcement. Now that I'm further along, it's easier to maintain my new mode of operation, but I still need the repetition, so the "default mode" doesn't slip back into gear. That can happen if I don't stay focused on the choice to simply *believe*. Recovery is a process, and faith is a process. This whole thing can be a little like learning how to ride a bicycle; you don't do it perfectly the first time. You work at it. Over and over again. But as I keep working it, I'm learning that He *can* do what I *can't* do.

The double blessing is that acting on faith and trust generates more faith and trust. The promises are true. As the *Big Book* says, "... we will comprehend the word serenity and we will know peace... We will intuitively know how to handle situations which used to baffle us. We will suddenly realize that God is doing for us what we could not do for ourselves."[15]

When I "came to believe" in December of 2013, the junk food bingeing stopped, my relationships started changing, and my mind and emotions started healing in double time. God was giving me my miracle. That doesn't mean my days were struggle free, but it does mean that there was progressive, consistent progress in every area. I have seen the love and power of God working for me, and it happens one day at a time as I continue to choose to believe. But I also know that if I choose *not* to believe on any given day, my insanity will be reinstated in about the same time it takes me to blink my eyes.

The great thing is: you find out pretty fast that a whole-hearted commitment to the Twelve Step program opens the door to the supernatural. God just gets involved in ways that you could never imagine, and the rewards are almost indescribable. I am truly grateful for this relationship with a Power greater than myself.

Because of Him, I'm not lost in the woods anymore.

Faith became my compass.

And *He* has become my True North.

Step Three:
I Did It My Way

BACK IN THE LATE SIXTIES, you didn't have to listen to the radio very long before hearing a Frank Sinatra tune called, "My Way." It became one of his signature songs and remains so to this day. I think the intention of the lyrics is to applaud individual authenticity, but my version of doing things "my way" had more to do with defiance. When I was in college, my mom questioned me one day as to why I acted in a particularly negative way.

My answer was, "That's just who I am."

... I was doing it *my way*.

In reality, I was shackled with so much shame that I couldn't bear to look inside and be honest with myself. And I sure didn't have the courage to admit my imperfections to someone else and ask for help in overcoming them. Of course, I didn't realize any of that at the time; walls of self-protection created a cognitive barrier. I sounded "tough" on the outside, but inside, I was as vulnerable as a baby bird. And didn't want to be. I resented it, so I covered it up with bravado. "That's just who I am." And all the while I was silently screaming, "I *hate* who I am."

Defiance is resistance. Sometimes defiance is for a good cause, and other times it's a measure of foolishness or emotional damage. So, you can call my defiance authenticity, or stupidity, or damage. But whatever it was, it wasn't creating the desired results. In *Twelve Steps and Twelve Traditions* of Alcoholics Anonymous, there is a reference to a psychological study concluding that defiance is, indeed, a primary characteristic of most or all alcoholics and addicts. I am no exception. In the days of my active addictions, my behavior and choices flew in the face of logic, good sense, and God. And even though I wasn't consciously trying to be that way, I was often in resistance.

Let me also say, however, that this was not my state of mind or heart every second of every day. At certain times, I could be sweet, compliant, thoughtful, and obedient. At other times, not so much. My behavior seemed to shift from one end of the spectrum to the other. There wasn't much happening in between. I was the swinging pendulum on a grandfather clock. But there is something I learned about God in the midst of it all ...

He never stopped loving me.

I'm bringing this up because it took me so very long to get to a place of *surrender*, and surrender was God's intended goal. Along the way, there were moments I was sure that He was completely disgusted with me. So, about the time I thought I was a horrible person, God would show me He was still there. When I would quiet my mind and listen to my heart, He was present. I could feel Him. Maybe He saw that I was trying to cross the river by "walking on water" all by myself. And maybe He knew that *I really did want to get this right*. Even when my behaviors were defiant, I can honestly say that I didn't want to be that way. I know that because I never completely gave in to the sin and sickness. I kept trying to stop. I kept trying to be different.

But I also know, now, that I wasn't trusting God, or myself, or anyone else to any great degree. Distrust can become a habit. And in spite of the fact that God had done miraculous things in my life, I continued to falter when it came to genuine trust. For the most part, I lived in a state of fear and anxiety. Maybe God was just giving me grace and a whole lot of extra time to come to grips with the real malady. When I look back over the years, it appears that He simply loved me enough to keep working with me. He didn't give up on me. He didn't let me go. He didn't withdraw His caring or His presence.

I can't begin to tell you how important that has become.

I had much to learn on my road to surrender. For one thing, I found out I didn't have a handle on real love. I also learned a lot about perceptions. Those perceptions, true or not, can create foundational beliefs that lead to choices that bring nothing but heartache and trouble. That was my experience. It's amazing to me how frequently we humans walk through life being pushed around by thoughts, ideas, and conclusions that are often below the surface of the conscious mind. And they become so rooted in the soil of our hearts that a "stronghold" is built. It becomes a wall of resistance to other ways of thinking and believing.

And *there*, we remain ... unless something comes along to shake things up enough to bring change.

The good news is: pain will shake you up.

I learned that, too.

Most, if not all, people in recovery will tell you that pain was their greatest motivator. We hit a wall of pain that reaches an unbearable level, and we start looking for an escape hatch. In some ways, it's like someone twisting your arm behind your back until you can't stand it anymore, and you yell, "Uncle!!" But in that very process, you find yourself opening your mind to other possible ways of living. And that is the prime reason why it's generally believed that an alcoholic or addict has to "hit bottom" in order to succeed. Frankly, when you don't have any other choice left, you will consider the "unpalatable."

... So, here's one choice I began to consider:

Step Three says: ***Made a decision to turn our will and our lives over to the care of God as we understood Him.***[16]

Surrender.

The frustrating thing is, I thought I started doing that in March of 1975 when I first got saved. I was genuinely trying to live the way I thought He wanted me to. That's the whole reason I chose to ask Jesus into my heart. I missed the part, however, where I needed to turn my *WILL* over to God. I kept trying to use my *WILL* power to stay away from bingeing, and much to my embarrassment and shame, I couldn't. It was horribly confusing. But, at the time, I just didn't know that obsessions, compulsions, and addictions don't respond to willpower.

So, even though my life definitely began to change for the better when I asked Jesus into my heart, I knew from the very beginning that I was not gaining victory over the habits and sins that haunted my daily living and kept me in a place of defeat. I hated that. There were times when I wondered if I was really a Christian. And other times when I wished I *wasn't* ... because comparing what my life WAS with what I knew it COULD be was often an exercise in torment. Something was missing. My Christian lifestyle was filled with "doing and striving," and there wasn't much of anything that felt like an easy yoke.

By the time I was three years into my Christian walk, my original "problem" was worse, and I had added a second "problem." I was going in the wrong direction. So, I stepped up my efforts and tried everything I knew to increase my willpower to get the sin out of my life, all to no avail. Why wasn't I free? I was trying my best to "fix" myself but kept falling into the same pit over and over again. It's a little baffling that I clung so long to the hope that I would one day wake up, and my nightmare would magically be over.

In, *The Language of Letting Go*, Melody Beattie helped me understand that life is a series of lessons that keep repeating until I finally comprehend and apply what is being taught.[17] In this particular instance, God, my loving Father, just kept repeating the lesson until I learned what I desperately needed to learn:

My way didn't work.

My way was to isolate, to trust in food, and to do it on my own. When I needed to let Jesus be my real Savior, I kept looking to food to fill the bill—which sounds extraordinarily ridiculous. But I had an established history with food. And even though it was a double-edged sword, food *did provide* a level of comfort, escape, and assistance—if you want to call it that. And then the other edge of the sword would take over and pour on the guilt, shame, and self-hatred, not to mention the pounds. The point is: I still trusted food to be there for me. I think I kept hoping I could eat all the food I wanted, with the benefit of temporary relief, without having to pay any consequences. But that's impossible. First of all, addiction is the disease of "more." You never get all you want; you always want *more*. Secondly, sin always has consequences. Lust, overindulgence, and idolatry are all sins. I couldn't possibly expect to get away with it. And I didn't.

Yes, indeed, my way didn't work.

If I could save myself, I wouldn't need Jesus. If my own willpower was enough to conquer addiction, I wouldn't need a Savior. If I could demolish sin in my own strength, I wouldn't need salvation purchased through the blood of God's Son. I had to learn that God just doesn't do things the same way I do them. He wants me to trust Him. He wants me to surrender. He wants me to turn my will over to Him.

Back in the mid-seventies, I read the powerful testimony of Nicky Cruz in his book, *Run Baby Run*. My remembrance of the story line is that Cruz, a drug-using gang member in New York City, heard about Jesus through Pastor David Wilkerson and made a decision to give his life to God. Nicky stopped using drugs and eventually became a Christian evangelist, but he did not have an overnight release from his addiction. The tormenting temptation still hit him at times. When it came, he apparently would fall on his face before God and pray until the intense pressure left.[18] I believe he had a handle on a very important concept: When you surrender to God in your weakness …

God can miraculously lift off the overpowering urge to sin.

It's nothing less than ironic that surrender brings power, but in God's world, that's how it works. Step Three is the Power Step. My part is to submit to God's will—daily, hourly, and moment by moment—following Him out of love and trust. God's part is to *empower* me to walk free from oppression, to heal my life, and to deliver me from temptation, which is exactly what He has promised to do. But, unless you're completely beaten down, this is a very tall order for the great majority of people living with addiction. Trust and surrender aren't usually common words in our vocabulary.

The thing about Twelve Step, though, is that God only asks us to be willing. Willing to trust. Willing to surrender. Willing to try something different—to take that one important step in His direction. You have to start somewhere. So, once I took a good look at my lack of choices and my thirty-eight years of living life my way, I finally became willing to do just that. It went something like this:

"God, I can't do this anymore."

"I surrender my will to You."

"I choose to trust You."

"I believe you can, and will, help me."

I was finished trying to be my own "god" and fix my own life. And I was finished putting my trust in food. By then, I knew that what I was doing with food was a dead-end street, so I was ready to give God a real chance—to get up every morning and say, "I'm willing to do this *Your* way, God. Your will be done, not mine."

And there you have Step Three.

Surrender works. And I have discovered that God is actually very gracious; He is easily approached. He is very willing to meet us where we are. But I have also noticed that, if I am struggling with a temptation, it's usually because I haven't surrendered my will in that moment, and I'm letting my mind *linger* on the desired substance or choice. Obviously, I am still sometimes tempted to trust food. But with a simple prayer it can all change: "God, I believe You love me, and I'm willing to live life Your way, not mine." When I mean it with all of my heart, the power shows up and the temptation "lifts off." However, the power does not come before the surrender. Sometimes the surrender and the power happen almost simultaneously, or sometimes I surrender and wait a short time, then the power shows up. But the power doesn't come first. I think that is God's way of waiting for me to choose to trust. And to reaffirm my belief in His love. This seems to be very important to Him. And I'm okay with that.

Lesson learned.

Now, the very last phrase of Step Three says, "God as we understood Him."

Those words were originally added to broaden the door for people with different religious beliefs and viewpoints, as is the use of "Higher Power" to identify one's object of faith. When AA first began, there was very little hope of recovery for most alcoholics and no viable recovery programs in sight. So, they were literally dealing with a life and death situation. I believe the AA founders, Bill Wilson and Dr. Bob, were simply trying to get people to walk through the door where they might find the tools of recovery instead of dying. They knew that a lot of folks resisted the Christian view of God due to misperceptions, negative experiences, or belonging to a differing faith. But it seems clear from their involvement with the Oxford Group, and as you read certain passages of the *Big Book*, that the founders knew Jesus as their Savior. Other contributing writers of the book also confirm their belief in our Heavenly Father through their personal testimonies.

The seriousness of the situation remains today; people still die from alcoholism and drug addiction. They die from food addiction as well. And a lot of folks, as they have previously "experienced" it, won't touch Christianity with a ten-foot pole. But they might walk through the door of a Twelve Step meeting. So, I don't have any problem "making the door larger." Once they get there, God can reveal all the truth He wants to reveal. You can't hear God's voice after you're dead.

I was someone who had no problem with Jesus being my Higher Power. The real problem was with my image of God. "God as I understood Him" was someone who could, or could not, be trusted. It all depended on certain factors. In the beginning of my Christian walk, my picture of God used to be pretty much like the view I had of my dad: unavailable, distant, preoccupied, and distracted. That put *me* in the position of being unimportant, unprotected, an oversight, and pretty much on my own. Unfortunately, I have discovered that I am not the only one who has faced this dilemma. A large number of people, even Christian people, wrestle with this unhelpful image of God. For me, I knew that change had to take place, or this whole new way of life wasn't going to work, and the addiction would remain. I also knew that the reasons for that faulty image needed to be addressed.

So, the journey began. And God started showing me who He really was and is. As with all things in the Twelve Step program, and with our relationship with God, it involves a process. A process is "a gradual change that leads to a particular result."[19] That says it perfectly. Part of this journey involved remembering past experiences and events where God purposefully showed me His love, His character, and His great willingness to work in my life. As I share one of these memories, my prayer is that you will begin to understand, if you don't already, that God is very interested in showing us that He's real, He's powerful, He *knows* us, and He cares to the utmost.

The story opens during my first year in full-time ministry. The challenges were huge, and it didn't take long for me to feel like I was drowning in an ocean of stress. Unfortunately, in many respects, it also felt like God didn't care. It *felt* like He just stood there with His arms crossed, watching me go through my battles, never lifting a hand to help. Toward the end of that time period, as the depression hit bottom and the anxiety became almost unbearable, I came very close to having a complete mental-emotional breakdown.

Surprisingly, instead of ending up in a mental institution ... my situation began to improve; I started feeling stronger, and I wasn't sure why. Needless to say, I was greatly relieved. But as time went on, I realized that I was holding on to feelings of hurt and anger toward God, even though I felt guilty doing so. My mind told me that my suspicions of His unfaithfulness weren't true, but my circumstances and feelings told me that He was not trustworthy. I quietly harbored this belief for quite some time, until one day, I read a scripture in Hebrews chapter 13 that brought the whole issue directly to the surface.

The words read: "God [God] Himself has said, I will not in any way fail you, *nor* give you up, *nor* leave you without support. [I will] not, [I will] not, [I will] not in any degree leave you helpless, *nor* forsake, *nor* let [you] down, [or even] (relax My hold on you)! [Assuredly not]! So, we take comfort *and* are encouraged *and* confidently *and* boldly say, The Lord is my Helper; I will not be seized with alarm ..." (Hebrews 13:5–6, AMPC).

As I read those verses, the tears started cascading like water on a slide. I finally poured out my heart to God and got honest about my feelings of betrayal. I even told Him that I knew the Word *said* He would never forsake me, but my emotions were telling me the exact opposite. When the painful words ran out, I waited with an open heart to listen to His response.

It came quickly. I didn't have to wait at all.

It was almost like *He* had been waiting months and years to finally have a chance to speak. He kindly, but firmly, said, "My Word is *true*. I want you to believe what My Word says instead of believing your feelings."

That was it. And the message was clear.

With His response, He showed me that I have the power to choose what I believe, and no one else can make that choice *for* me. But my foundational beliefs about God, and my image of Him, need to come from His Word and not from my negative emotions.

That choice is in front of me, Word or emotions, every day.

How I choose to see God is a choice in front of me as well.

So, my story of "learning who God really was and is" has a good ending. As I chose to believe in God's faithfulness, He revealed to me all the ways that He had blessed me and helped me during that first year of full-time ministry when I felt so alone. I'll share just three of them: 1) He brought my best friend into my life that year, a woman who loved me unconditionally for over three decades until the time of her passing; 2) God showed me that He fought against the enemy on my behalf in ways of which I was completely unaware; and 3) unbeknownst to me, He supernaturally spoke to an elderly couple *in Minnesota* to pray for me during the year of my mental-emotional descent. They had never met me, but their story is that God gave them "only a name" ... and they knew they were to pray for a woman named "Kim" on a daily basis.

At the end of that year, at a Washington D.C. convention, God brought the three of us together—this elderly couple and me—and revealed the whole story. It was after many months of their consistent prayers that I had finally started feeling better. I shudder to think of what might have happened without their intercession. To this day, I am amazed at their willingness to pray for a complete stranger only by name and God's faithfulness in asking them to do so. The sweet icing on the cake was the way He supernaturally unveiled the story, confirming the depth of His love. In truth, God had never left me at all. He had been there continuously, working on my behalf.

And He still is.

It has taken some time, but I have come to strongly believe in the love of my Heavenly Father. That belief began as an act of faith and was positively reinforced with every miraculous step toward healing and recovery that He orchestrated in response. I have come to understand that how I "see" Him affects my ability to give my will and my life over to His care. So, for me, one of the keys to Step Three is actively believing in His wisdom, goodness, and power. I choose to believe, and I choose to surrender my will and my life to Him, because of that wisdom, goodness, and power. Every day that I live life with sanity and sobriety testifies to the strength of that choice.

It's simple. But it works.

You just have to be willing.

All I know is ... if you choose to trust in that love,

you'll come face-to-face with a God who will never let you go.

Step Four:
From Pain ... to Peace

HER NAME WAS ANN.

On the day that I realized God had handpicked this woman and orchestrated our spiritual collaboration, gratitude washed over me like a tidal wave. She was no less than a Godsend. When I met Ann, I was desperate enough to ask for help, but I was also emotionally fragile. I had tried counseling before and quickly learned that the style and personality of a counselor can make a big difference. I couldn't handle "straight and blunt." What someone else considered "sharing information" sometimes came across as condemnation and criticism. My personal filters were clogged with shame, and I would walk out of the session feeling worse than when I arrived. It turns out I needed someone who listened quietly, responded gently, and covered it all with unconditional acceptance.

That was Ann.

She had a kindness about her that made me feel cared for and a demeanor that generated trust and a sense of safety. I was a co-pastor and a worship leader living a double life at the time—and very much dealing with the belief that if anyone really knew me ... they wouldn't like me. Besides, as a pastor, I thought I was "supposed to have it all together" and not be in need of counseling in the first place. My protective walls were as high as the Empire State Building. So, it was going to take a major dose of "safe" to get me to divulge the stories packed away in my secret closets. She knew that instinctively. She knew it had taken a lot of pain to get me into her office. She went slowly. She was very thoughtful with the words she spoke and highly aware of my sensitivity. She was the perfect fit.

The interesting thing is, God had already "talked to me" about entering into a healing process and finding the help I needed. In July of that year, while we were on vacation in North Carolina, He used a verse during my morning quiet time that created a deep, lasting impact. I knew that those exact words were being spoken to me by His Spirit.

The verse says, "... Be strong and courageous and get to work. Don't be frightened by the size of the task, for the Lord my God is with you; he will not forsake you. He will see to it that everything is finished correctly" (1 Chronicles 28:20, TLB).

When I read those words, I knew instantly that God was talking to me about emotional healing. The inner knowing was so strong that it reverberated on the inside of me for about twenty minutes. It was an actual physical sensation as well as a spiritual guidepost that I will never forget. I knew God was placing this task before me and that He would help me. I had some sense of how big it was going to be, but I also knew that I would not be alone. I was ready.

Four months later, I was sitting in Ann's office.

It's a good thing that God promised to walk with me because those hours of counseling were like diving headfirst into a murky lake where you can't see what's below the surface. As we met for our weekly appointments, I sometimes felt like a small child crossing a busy street, still wanting someone to hold my hand. Or a Midwest teenager lost in a big city. Sometimes there were moments of grief that felt like a crushing weight and other times an anger so intense that I shook all over. That's what happens when you stuff your emotions for decades. And that's why God provided a safe place for the process. At the end of most of our weekly sessions, headway had been made. I often went home, however, and had a binge afterward—unconsciously overwhelmed by the fear of revealing who I was. Rejection seemed inevitable.

But she surprised me.

She liked me. I could feel it. And she took me just the way I was — good, bad, and ugly— without pointing out my faults. She knew I was pretty good at doing that myself. The longer I went to those sessions, the safer I felt, and that led to nothing but good. I was finally able to talk about every aspect of the abortion, all the pent-up feelings toward my parents, a lot of the fears, the hurtful experiences in ministry, and much more. She listened to it all and often had perceptive responses that helped me look at people, situations, and myself from a different viewpoint. A helpful viewpoint.

My daughter calls it "reframing."

And what a good word that is. Sometimes we get stuck thinking about a person or event in one particular, and negative, way. Reframing involves removing the old, familiar parameters and applying the new. Like: "My dad was critical, rigid, and distant when I was a girl" turns into "My dad was following the example set for him by his father." It changes the look of the entire "painting." And that often leads to the treasure at the end of the journey: Acceptance.

Acceptance doesn't mean that what happened was okay. It means it has been dealt with—the feelings have been felt. The pain has been acknowledged by someone else. The power to inflict has been removed. Self-examination has become a positive tool instead of a flogging whip. Understanding comes; forgiveness is released. And you enter a place of rest. It may not follow that exact course every time; but for me, it's usually pretty close.

So, during those many months with Ann, and without me knowing it, I was walking through Step Four (and Step Five) but calling it by another name: counseling. The end result was the same. Troublesome issues were resolved, shame was diminished, and I was moving toward a greater level of wholeness. Going to see a counselor was not the only venue God gave me for Step Four, but it was one of the most significant. The point is: I found a trustworthy person to talk to. You will need to do the same. Whether it's a sponsor, a counselor, or a friend who has become a safe haven ... I pray you will find a "place" where you can share who you really are.

One of the initial challenges, however, lay in my need to "learn to talk." Talking about my inner life wasn't something familiar or practiced. In fact, my belief was if I didn't talk about something, it would go away. If I kept something a secret, it would simply disappear. But nothing could be further from the truth. Holding those secrets inside makes them sprout like poisonous mushrooms and increases their power to dish out all varieties of emotional pain. As human beings, we even have this incredible ability to mentally block out portions of our lives. It's as though we place the memories in a black, thick-walled box, securely attach the lid, and sequester the parcel on a high, hard-to-reach shelf. That ability is useful when we don't have the tools to deal with the pain, but it doesn't work interminably. Sooner or later, the issues come to the surface—and often at inconvenient moments when exposure is undesirable. Or they come out in hurtful ways toward others that we don't even recognize.

Ultimately, the secrets have to be uncovered, examined, and exorcised.

If we want to get well.

Having said all that, it's perfectly understandable why this Step can create anxiety in the hearts of those committed to recovery. The Fourth Step says: ***Made a searching and fearless moral inventory of ourselves.***[20] And, in plain and simple language ... this Step is difficult. But, although it can create a certain amount of discomfort in the working, a tremendous healing awaits those who complete their Fourth Step journey—one that can be equaled by no other.

It's a life-changer.

When I was in fifth grade playing outside during recess, I fell on some sand-covered asphalt next to the school baseball diamond. Picking myself up, I looked down at my leg and saw that it was covered with blood, dirt, and grit. The pain was intense from the scrape that extended for about six inches between my knee and ankle. When I went home and had my mom help me clean up the injured area, it was very sensitive to any kind of touch, and I just wanted to hurry up and be done with it. She completed her first aid and covered the area with gauze in an effort to keep it clean, but a few days later when I checked, it was red with inflammation, and yellow pus was oozing from the open wound where the outer layer of skin had been scraped off. There was obviously embedded, foreign material that had not yet been removed. Now, the cleansing process was even more painful due to the infection, but it had to be done in order for my leg to heal. I'm happy to say that the wound was thoroughly cleaned, an antibacterial was applied, the pain was endured, the leg healed ... and the subsequent scar even faded after several years.

Here's the point: there isn't anyone working through the Twelve Steps who hasn't been wounded by people, events, and/or circumstances. We have all been injured mentally, emotionally, spiritually, socially, and sometimes physically and/or sexually. I believe this is true for all people, to one degree or another, because that's just what happens when we live in this world. So, there are reasons why we are angry, reasons why we are depressed, reasons why we are afraid, reasons why we act out compulsively, and reasons why we try to control, work hard to fix everybody, and become addicted to substances, people, and behaviors. Nobody is really exempt. But the good news is that God knows what those reasons are, and He does not leave us in our pain, unless we choose to stay there. What He wants for us is healing.

Just like my scraped leg had to be cleaned out in order for the skin and tissues to regenerate, God wants to reach into the brokenness of our souls and cleanse them from the damage that has occurred. This healing forms a sure foundation for the regeneration of our lives.

In a nutshell: If you want "new" life, you have to deal with the "old."

The difficulty lies in the fact that those parts of our lives and hearts in need of healing are super sensitive. We don't want to touch them because it hurts when we do. So, we avoid the pain like it was "the plague," not realizing that hanging on to that pain is what pushes us toward addiction. But all the Steps, including Step Four, are designed to navigate us from troubled waters into the seas of tranquility. I have come to believe that whatever God wants me to see and acknowledge, even if painful, is for my benefit and my good. Acknowledgment is a required step in the protocol. If I try to keep something a secret, it holds my heart captive and takes me prisoner. But whatever I bring to the light [of God] will be *made light* from exposure to HIS light (Ephesians 5:13, AMPC). Without examination and cleansing, we live with the effects of moral and emotional inflammation and infection.

This is also confirmed in Proverbs 4:23, which states it in a different and very powerful way: "Guard your heart above all else, for it determines the course of your life" (Proverbs 4:23, NLT).

What I gleaned from that verse is that I need to make the state of my heart an extremely high priority—to assess it, to guard it from evil, to nurture it, and to ask for God's help in addressing any weakness and/or brokenness. The state of my heart actually determines the choices I make; it determines the direction and the pathway upon which I travel through life, whether it's for good or for bad. Simply said, when my heart is broken and wounded, I make broken choices that lead to further unhappiness. But when my heart is healed, I make healthy choices that lead me to joy and usefulness in the hands of God.

And this is what Step Four is all about.

Knowing how very important this is, God may have already led you to people and resources that have inspired some sort of Fourth Step process. And don't be surprised if He did. Hindsight has revealed to me a multitude of events where God stepped in and orchestrated His will in my life without me even asking. Sometimes God does His will in spite of us. He's been running the universe for a long time, and I have discovered He's quite good at it. He requires my cooperation at certain intervals, but He's pretty capable of getting things done. So, when my Father knew that I was getting ready to start the healing process, He helped to get the ball rolling. You see, it took fourteen years of bingeing to get me to even admit to myself that I needed outside assistance. But once I made the admission, something shifted on the inside.

I wanted to get well.

The year was 1987, and we were on a vacation in Virginia Beach; my husband, myself, and our two kids. I was an absolute mess. I wanted to eat everything in sight, and I wanted to eat all day long, every day. There were a couple of times, while Jason took the kids to the beach, that I stayed in the hotel room and ordered room service, so I could binge on French fries. I lied so I could stay behind ... said I wasn't feeling well.

By then, I was also starting to have adverse physical side effects from the fourteen years of bingeing, and at times, needed to stay close to a restroom. To say it mildly, I wrecked the vacation for myself, and I didn't do my husband or kids any favors either. Addiction is selfish, sinful, and sick. What can I say? Five days into the week, I was alone in the room once again and had an epiphany: something was wrong with me.

… Go figure.

It was such an eye-opener that I actually called a local ministry in Virginia Beach, hoping to get a last-minute appointment with a counselor—but there weren't any openings. That was the first time I sought help. Denial had ruled the day up until then. I didn't need outside help; I just needed to stay on a diet and lose weight. Don't let anyone tell you that denial isn't real. It's not only real; it's powerful. I had completely surrounded myself with delusions and deceptions.

But the seed had been planted. Within ten months, I started going to support groups, and God started working with me in very direct ways. What I have learned about God is this: if you take a half-step in His direction, He will draw on all the resources of heaven and the universe to meet you there. God saw me opening myself just a little to the prospect of getting well, and He started doing things that took my breath away.

For instance: I had a big brown recliner in our living room where I had quiet time every morning: coffee and "communion" with God. On one particular day when I was especially tired, I pulled my knees up under me and turned sideways, so I could nestle into the back of the chair, almost in a fetal position. I had only been curled up for a minute when I started feeling a warm glow all around me. My eyes were closed, and suddenly it felt like I was a child sitting on someone's lap … God's lap. He slowly wrapped His arms around me as I was leaning against His shoulder and held me so tenderly that the tears started flowing. Not sad tears—tears of amazement and gratitude. I could feel this powerful love, and it was flowing from Him right into my body. I wasn't just imagining it; I could physically feel something covering me and moving through me, gently and sweetly. Something comforting, assuring, and real.

God was loving on me.

And I could hear these quiet words on the inside of me promising, "You can stay here as long as you like. I won't push you away or tell you it's time to stop. I will hold you just as long as you want me to. You can come back anytime you like, and I will be here."

Can you imagine what that did to my heart? That was the first day I remember crossing over the line from trying to change myself, unsuccessfully, to letting God do what I didn't realize He could do. The truth was, He not only could—He had a very strong desire to do so. And I had been clueless. I later realized that He was holding me on His lap like I had wanted my parents to hold me when I was young.

The healing had begun.

God has so many ways of healing our hearts that we don't have enough books in this world to write them all down. He made each of us unique, so He deals with us in unique ways—ways that are personally tailored to our needs and our personality ... and our damage. I didn't ask God to come into my living room that day and start healing my heart. But I had been opening myself to change, and He just showed up. I can assure you that I went back to that chair many, many times to let Him hold me, and each time I did, He reaffirmed His powerful love.

Have I mentioned that love heals?

If I already have, let me say it again: love heals.

I had no idea that God could do something like that—just step into your life in a supernatural way and give you what you didn't even realize you needed most. But that's who God is. He's a Father. He's a Lover. He's a Nurturer. He's a Healer.

A minister once took my hands in his and kindly told me that God was going to "soften my approach to life." I didn't really know what he was referring to at the time, but I know now. My view of life was pretty hard. My view of God wasn't much better. I have sometimes wondered why God touched me in some of the supernatural ways that He did, but I think He was "softening my approach to life."

I've heard stories from Jewish people who have had encounters with Jesus where He literally showed up and revealed Himself to them in a personal way to let them know He is truly the Messiah. Sometimes we have such resistant walls on the inside of us that it takes a special event to pull them down. This is how God has dealt with me at times. He has shown up in very personal ways because He knows that's what I need. And He loves me enough to meet that need.

How very gracious and merciful He is.

I've talked a lot about healing, so now let's take a closer look at the portion of Step Four that helps us get there: the inventory. The exercise of looking inside ourselves (an inventory) must begin with a commitment to honesty. It's pretty useless without that element. An inventory is about seeking Truth, facing Truth, and dealing in Truth. God's Word teaches us that Truth is innately strong and enduring, so, it follows suit that if honesty brings us to Truth, honesty will take us to very good places. Jesus declared that Truth sets us free, and He knew what He was talking about. As we build our new lives in recovery, the components of honesty and truth actually become the foundational support for all that follows. Without these two pillars, there is nothing substantial upon which to build, and the freedom we seek will be fleeting, if it exists at all.

The *Big Book* says in chapter five, "Rarely have we seen a person fail who has thoroughly followed our path. Those who do not recover are people who cannot or will not completely give themselves to this simple program, usually men and women who are constitutionally incapable of being honest with themselves."[21]

An honest inventory opens the door to healing.

And healing will give birth to freedom.

Because of that, one of my greatest desires is that you would not let fear stop you from your Fourth Step journey. Whatever God needs you to see will be taken care of. He will only show you what you are ready to see. And He will only show you when He knows you are ready to receive His healing touch. He is so completely trustworthy in this. He just needs you to be willing to take a look inside yourself, so the work can begin.

One word to the wise: watch out for shame and don't try to do this Step totally on your own. This is not a solo flight. Addicted people usually live with some level of shame; we innately recognize that what we are doing isn't good. Then we make what we Do ... who we Are. This leads to a whole new set of problems surrounding our self-image and state of mind. My past tendency was to be extremely hard on myself; I was often my own worst enemy and could focus on my faults to the point of despair. But I have found that God's image of me is much more merciful and well-rounded. He doesn't expect me to be perfect. He expects me to move toward progress, recognizing that there will always be something about me that needs improvement. And that's okay. The Bible states that God doesn't change (Malachi 3:6, NLT), but I have learned He is a Master at changing me. This is actually His promise. So, what helps me is to pray for a vision of how God sees me, to pray for the strength to acknowledge the good instead of automatically rejecting it (and some of you know what I'm talking about), and to pray for the revelation that He accepts ALL of me. Ultimately, as we work Step Four, we are empowered to come "out of darkness into His marvelous light" (1 Peter 2:9, AMPC). Then He is the one who is glorified, and it is glory that He deserves.

I didn't really know what I was doing when I did my first actual Fourth Step, but I was purposing to follow the Twelve Step program, and I believe God honored that effort. He will do the same with you. In the many years since then, I've gone through at least six seasons of working on my personal inventory and seeking God's healing and growth in my life in very intentional ways. Intense but good. And on occasion, I also do a short Fourth and Fifth Step with my sponsor, or trusted friend, to deal with a particular issue that comes to the surface. For instance, when these three areas were brought to my attention, I did a mini-Fourth Step in regard to: insecurity, defensiveness, and a critical attitude. I wrote out how those particular character defects had shown up in my life and shared the results with my sponsor who gave helpful feedback and input. ALL of the inventory work that I have ever done has helped me to grow spiritually and emotionally, and regret has never been included. Only gratitude.

Most of us who have a few years under our belts will agree that the good things in life are worth a little effort. Sometimes they are worth a *lot* of effort. So, I have chosen to do whatever it takes to find the daily treasures of peace and freedom, in spite of any hardship. The greatest motivator for change that I have ever experienced is feeling enough pain that I'm willing to do whatever it takes to NOT feel it anymore. That's what got me through my multiple workings of Step Four, and it was pain well-utilized.

It's easy to get overwhelmed with this Step. But, one of the identifying hallmarks of the Twelve Step program is the concept of breaking things down—for example: taking life one day at a time. This practical guideline can be extremely helpful in doing a personal inventory. Take baby steps. Cut it up into bite-size pieces. Don't stuff the whole steak into your mouth and try to chew. I have learned the hard way that I can take a quick glance at the overall project in front of me, but when it looks huge, I need to back off and divide it into whatever is manageable. That sometimes comes with some trial and error, but eventually I figure it out.

A personal inventory can be much the same.

What is manageable for you? Maybe a good start is writing about one person who had a significant impact on your life. Or taking a single character defect, like stubbornness, and writing how that has manifested in your work and relationships. Whatever you can think of is okay. Really. This is not a contest. This is about getting well. And if you pray and ask God to partner with you as you go, then He can and will assist you in amazing ways.

If you are facing Step Four, please remember that there are a variety of resources available to guide us through this process successfully. A lot of the self-examination will be done in private, but invaluable support can be yours through the involvement of other Twelve Steppers and by consistently asking for God's wisdom and direction. So, if you find yourself shaking in your boots at the prospect of a moral inventory, there are three things you can do: 1) you can ask God for willingness; 2) you can ask Him for courage; and 3) you can ask for advice from a "veteran" at a Twelve Step meeting. Since the Father wants you to be healed, I can guarantee that assistance will come. This all may feel new, strange, and awkward, but the question is:

Do you want to be free?

There may be a price for freedom ... but the freedom is well worth the price.

Step Five:
Soul Cleansing

SOME THINGS IN LIFE are just meant to go together ... like puppies and smiles, movies and popcorn, and hammock swings and naps. Steps Four and Five go together in pretty much the same way, except on a more serious note. First, *we make a fearless, moral inventory of ourselves*, which is Step Four; then *we admit to God, to ourselves, and to another human being the exact nature of our wrongs*, which is Step Five.[22] The idea is to verbally share the discoveries we have made about ourselves in Step Four, whether it's a character defect, the pain of a traumatic event, unproductive reactions to life, or something *positive* that we didn't see before. Although Step Five is different, this Step can be almost as intimidating as the previous one, and most people carry it out with some level of trepidation. So, in light of that, you might be asking, "Can't I just think about this stuff in my head? Why do I need to make such a big deal out of it?"

Those are good questions.

When I first shared an overview of how the Twelve Steps work in my life, I mentioned that the healing journey can be broken down into four different areas. Steps One, Two, and Three focus on our relationship with God; Steps Four through Seven are about settling things with *ourselves*; Steps Eight and Nine are about resolving relationships with *others*; and Steps Ten through Twelve are about keeping the positive ball rolling. So, Steps Four and Five are designed to help us come to a place of peace in regard to who we are and what we have done ... or sometimes *haven't* done. Most of us can recognize and admit that we have *not* been at peace with ourselves. This peace is a very important goal of recovery. It comes from God, holds us steady, and keeps us anchored in Him. And since emotional stress is often a catalyst for acting out addictively, peace becomes a high priority in our new way of living.

In the past, the major source of my agitation, fear, and self-hatred came from the choices I had made in life and the view I had of myself in light of those choices. Rest assured; my view was not good. The loss of innocence in spirit, soul, and body at the age of seventeen threw me into a downward spiral that was crowned by the inward belief that I was a murderer and didn't deserve to live. This belief was a deep, dark secret that I shared with no one, so the guilt and shame that I carried on the inside were like arsenic eating at my soul. Not knowing God, or His forgiveness, this poisonous state of mind and emotion led directly to compulsive food bingeing—a conscious choice, subconsciously meant to be an antidote.

But my sin was "ever before me," as Psalm 51 says, continually raising its ugly head to pronounce my guilt (Psalm 51:3, AMPC). I lived in almost perpetual shame for the next twenty years, between the ages of eighteen and thirty-eight. And even though I had come to know the Lord during that time, I struggled with receiving His forgiveness—and especially with forgiving myself.

Guilt is a heavy burden to carry. It's a millstone tied around our necks topped off by a blanket of condemnation. And condemnation brings us under judgment, with little or no hope of absolution. Legitimate guilt can and should be addressed, and God has made a way to do that through Jesus. But many of us have wrestled with the logistics. Sometimes there are confusing complications.

As for shame—shame was the voice in my head that told me I was a BAD person. Not just what I had done ... but who I actually was in the core of my being. Or at least, who I believed I was. Shame was the muddied filter through which I looked at myself. And instead of realizing that the mud was stuck to the filter, I thought the mud was part of me. That created depression and hopelessness. I have come to believe that shame is evil, and I wouldn't wish it on anyone. Maybe you have noticed, as I have, that guilt and shame can turn us into people that God never created us to be.

Way too many years of my life were spent grappling with the effects of self-condemnation and self-hatred; the by-products of guilt and shame. And with that came the need to hide. I hid from others, and I hid from myself. And, I suppose I was also trying to hide from God. As created beings, we humans seem to be very self-protective, which for me, often manifested in denying the truth. I didn't want to see who I was. I was expecting to see the worst, and I didn't want to look. It was so easy to look somewhere else and avoid the confrontation. So, it took me a long time to gather the courage to go through this discomfort.

And then, the other side of the coin was realizing that pride was "alive and well" in the pages of my life story, which was something I didn't really want to admit. Step Five seemed undesirable because I didn't want anyone to see my imperfections. Gee, I had worked really hard all of my life to cover them up and make myself look as perfect as possible. But pride is an isolator by nature; it separates us from each other and fights against the divine goal of living in genuine community. So, I began to see the need to push past this stumbling block and find a heart of humility.

Meanwhile, as I procrastinated, staying "hidden" wasn't all that hard to do. For instance, isolation is an excellent way to save yourself from exposure. Just limit the amount of time that you spend around other people, and it's easy to hide who you are and what you have done. In my years of going to Twelve Step groups, I have found that isolation, as a means of hiding, is the hands-down favorite of addicted folks. The only problem is that God created us to need other people, and in the effort to hide, a primary human need goes unmet. So, it actually creates pain that feeds back into the addiction. No surprise there.

Most or all addicts are also looking for "permission" to use, and isolation has a way of generating a pseudo-permission slip to engage in the addictive behavior or activity. There's no accountability. My dad used to drive out into the country and find a solitary spot to drink vodka right up to the point where he almost couldn't drive home. Then he would return to the house and fall asleep in his recliner. As for me, my favorite time to read romance books and binge on junk food was, of course, when no one else was around. Somewhere in my mind I knew that God could see me, but it's much easier to ignore Someone who is invisible than someone who is not.

Then, there's the other kind of isolation where you're not alone in social terms; like drinking at a bar or doing drugs at a party. But you are alone in regard to genuine relationship and connection with other human beings. And when you use your substance around other folks who are doing the same, there is, again, a pseudo-permission slip to do exactly what you're doing. Everyone else is doing it, so it must be okay, right?

There is also an element of hiding in the actual substance abuse. We often get to be "someone else" when we are using. We might let our hair down or become the life of the party or suddenly turn into the best joke-teller on the planet. Or conveniently forget about who we are.

But we're still hiding.

I hid from my feelings by pushing them down with food. I also hid from myself by "becoming the heroine" of a romance novel. Being beautiful, slender, accomplished, and in love is a profile highly desired by most women. And it certainly sounded good to me. If I could temporarily pretend to be someone else, to live vicariously through them, I could gain a few precious hours of relief. Relief, however, that never lasted longer than the end of the book.

Ultimately, hiding is about fear. Fear of rejection, fear of failure, fear of success, fear of never being who you really want to be, fear of feeling a multitude of uncomfortable emotions that you would rather avoid, and fear of someone figuring out that you're not who you pretend to be. In the end ... it doesn't work. It backfires. Because you can't hide from yourself forever.

And you can never hide from God.

So, Step Five is about coming out of hiding in order to find peace.

And in order to find peace, I have to deal with the guilt and shame. It's as simple and as complicated as that. Even before my commitment to Twelve Step, I started asking God to teach me about this topic. And He did. One of the things He revealed to my heart many years ago was that I had to be ready to release the guilt in my life. For example, the guilt I held onto for about ten years after leaving the ministry and going through with the divorce that followed. I believed with all of my heart that ministry was my calling—yet, I left. As for divorce, I did not believe in it and never thought I would choose to do such a thing. But I did. And I lived with "heaviness" because of those choices.

Until I finally got tired of it.

God sometimes waits for us to get tired of things we carry around in life. Then, when He knows we're ready, He "parts the curtain" and shows us the answer. That's exactly what He did in this instance. The "unveiling" revealed that I was hanging on to my guilt for two specific reasons: 1) because I thought I didn't deserve forgiveness, and 2) because I was using guilt to punish myself and try to pay penance. Both of those reasons totally negate the work that Jesus accomplished on the cross. The truth is: I didn't deserve forgiveness. No one does. God forgives me because Jesus paid the price for all of my sin and wrongdoing. I can't earn forgiveness because it's a gift. And, as far as punishing myself... why in the world would I try to pay penance when I'm powerless to meet the demand? I don't know. I can't pay any kind of price to make my sin okay with God. There's only one way out of sin, and that's through repentance and receiving the work of the cross. Jesus took my punishment. Those are some of the Revealed Truths that I finally saw and incorporated into my life, and when I did, the guilt rolled off of my back like a two-ton sack of cement.

You can count it as fact that God wants to help us resolve our internal conflicts that make us feel guilty and ashamed.

He knows what that kind of soul-cleansing will do for us.

And, as with most things that I've been afraid of in life, my soul-cleansing wasn't nearly as brutal as I thought it might be.

To simplify: the overarching goal of recovery is to change the negative to positive. We don't have lasting sobriety without that transformation. And one of the greatest benefits of the Fifth Step is the end result: a "one-eighty" change in how we feel about ourselves. People can be crippled in so many different ways by their self-image. It can keep you from success, from reaching your potential, and from even making the effort to try. It can keep you from enjoying what you do accomplish. It can keep you from socializing, from being comfortable in a multitude of situations, and from reaching out to others. It can keep you from giving love, receiving love, and believing in love. And it can keep you from having joy and experiencing any kind of real peace.

Because addiction creates shame, what we believe about ourselves needs a new and fresh beginning. Through my years of active addiction, there were lots of people who said good things about me and showed gratitude for the help they received as God utilized my gift-ings. But unfortunately, what mattered most was the way I felt about myself. What was buried inside was a slow-releasing, subtle poison from a bottomless pit. The kudos from doing something good, or having a particular talent, would keep me from total despair, but praise and "applause" didn't make any permanent dent in my negative self-perceptions. To keep my head above water, I would just move on to the next opportunity to do something that got a few more kudos. Folks are sometimes shocked when they hear of a highly gifted, rich, or famous person committing suicide. We wonder why someone with financial resources, notoriety, or so much potential would feel the need to take their own life. We think because we see them in a certain positive light that, surely, they do too. But look at people like Robin Williams, Ernest Hemingway, Vincent Van Gogh, and Tony Scott (the director of *Top Gun*).

Clearly, that is not the case.

The perception of who and what we are is very personal and often very private.

It's also very important.

The best and most accurate image of who I am, however, needs to come from God. And, in order to see myself the way God sees me, I have to come out of hiding. Otherwise, I can never be who He created me to be. As long as I keep hiding … I stay stuck.

When I think about it now, what seems clear to me is that God has placed certain desires on the inside of us. I believe they are innate; we are born with them. And one of them is to BE who God created each one of us to be and to feel good about ourselves. Not prideful, but content. This is the nature of God. Do you think God sits around feeling depressed about the way He looks, or allows fear to hold Him back from helping someone? I don't think so. This may sound a little ridiculous, but I think God likes who He is. And I think He wants me to have the same contentment. When I don't, something doesn't feel right. On some level, don't we recognize that we're missing the mark when we feel a certain way and do certain things? Isn't there something on the inside of us that keeps pointing to God's desires for us and God's image of us? I think there is. And I think the sooner we choose to put God in charge and live life His way—and choose to see ourselves the way He sees us—the sooner we will find the resolution to our conflicting choices and enjoy the inner tranquility that inevitably follows.

In Psalm 51, David says: "You desire truth in the inner being ... Create in me a clean heart, O God, and renew a right, persevering, *and* steadfast spirit within me" (Psalm 51:6,10, AMPC).

This is a prayer with an answer to be joyfully anticipated!

Hearing and receiving Truth is what creates a clean heart and a steady spirit. It also renews our minds, ushering us into lasting change. And isn't change what we are all looking for ... change that brings freedom?

Many people have said that Step Five is where they first sensed the grace of God moving into their lives to lift the addiction, the obsession, the fear, and the condemnation. Maybe that's because this Step significantly helps to clear away the debris from our past, which changes the topography of our souls. It just makes us feel better. It's kind of like coming in for a hot shower after getting all dirty and sweaty working out in the yard. Getting clean feels good. Confession, as part of soul-cleansing, has been around for centuries because it clearly leads to a place of acceptance and the resolution of sin.

I have done several Fourth and Fifth Steps, with each effort creating what I call "a shedding experience." This is where I let go of another layer of old, dirty, grimy stuff that was keeping me weighed down like brick and mortar. And yes, verbally sharing all of these things out loud is an important part of the Step. I have been amazed by what God has revealed to me when I have spoken about an issue out loud, in place of just thinking about it in my head or silently praying to the Lord. Hearing something with your own ears makes a difference; it simply registers on the heart and mind in a different way. And often leads to an "aha moment." These revelations have always moved me toward freedom, and I think maybe God gives these insights as a reward for our obedience. And just because He loves us so much. God has spent many years healing different areas of my life, and what He promised has come true. For quite a while now, I have been waking up in the morning actually liking who I am. The way I feel about myself has gone through a dramatic turnaround, which then created, and still creates, inner joy and a place of Rest.

... THIS is how God wants us to live.

Some time ago, as I was preparing to do my first Fifth Step, I began to notice how specifically it is written. It says to "admit to God, to ourselves, and to another human being the exact nature of our wrongs."

So, why do we have to admit this stuff three times in three different ways? Another good question. And here's how I break that down: I admit my wrongs to God because confession clears the path to forgiveness and release. I admit my wrongs to myself because I can't cooperate with God's changes in my life until I SEE what needs to change. Clearly, we lean toward denial and blindness in regard to our faults. Then, I admit my wrongs to another human being for two reasons: 1) to know that I'm loved and accepted in spite of my imperfections, and 2) to get feedback from a person who can help me gain new perspectives.

Thus, choosing the right person to hear your Step Five is a key element. Addictions have a way of twisting things around in our minds. Our views become skewed. So, it's important to walk out Step Five with someone we trust, and someone who has some experience and can speak balance and wisdom into our lives. Someone who can help us see ourselves through God's eyes. We might be surprised at what God sees.

In the recent past, I did a Fifth Step confession in regard to a choice I made two years prior. After I had made this particular choice, I found it hard to stay in a place of peace with myself and God. I asked God to forgive me. I forgave myself. I made amends to the others involved. But I still couldn't get a handle on consistent, lasting peace. In short: it kept bugging me. You know what I'm talking about? So, I took it to my pastor with the intent of doing a Step Five, thinking that's what I needed for closure. But, for his own reasons, he stopped me from sharing the details. He just wanted to know the gist of the issue and move on to a solution.

At first, I was fine with that and thought the saddle burr had been removed, but then the same guilt began to resurface once again. I came against the enemy, placed the past under the blood of Jesus, and reminded myself that God "has removed our sins as far from us as the east is from the west" (Psalm 103:12, NLT). I did everything I knew to do. I even had an opportunity to share a portion of the issue with a friend and thought maybe that would be the end of it. But it wasn't. The guilt continued to recycle.

Finally, I realized that I was going to have to bite the bullet.

I needed to do a thorough and complete Step Five with someone I trusted, so God showed me who to ask, and I set up the appointment.

I found myself feeling anxious and ashamed, but I learned long ago to not let that stop me. I prayed for courage and went through with it.

The person I talked to was the perfect choice to hear my confession. Her kindness, wisdom, and Biblical input was just what I needed. There was no judgment; she just made it easy for me to sit down and share all that was necessary to share. And then her response was truthful, straightforward, and compassionate. As she helped me look at the situation through God's eyes and closed out our time with prayer, I knew that the spiritual seal had been put on the issue once and for all. Even before I exited the building, a fountain of joy had already begun to bubble up on the inside of me. When you carry the burden of guilt and shame around for a long period of time, the release of it is sweet, indeed. With this one, I could almost physically feel God lifting the weight from my shoulders and removing the heaviness from my soul.

And I think what I love the most is realizing all over again that God doesn't want me to carry these burdens around interminably. He's not trying to punish me. He wants me to follow His guidelines for dealing with the sin so I can be free from it. Lay it down. Put it away. Move on.

And that's just what I did.

I haven't been bothered by it since then. The peace remains; I feel right with myself and right with my Father.

God knew what He was doing with Step Five.

And even though this Step can be a challenge, I hope you have, or are getting, the revelation that it is truly needful. Nobody said the Steps were easy. They just said that if you do them, you'll find a daily reprieve from addiction and the soul-sickness through which it is generated. Step Five brings us to a place of positive change because it brings us into the presence of God. It's a place of healing where the loud voices of condemnation dissipate, and we are finally at rest.

I know this because I have experienced it. It really does work ... if you work it.

Step Six:
The Principle of Preparation

OVER THE YEARS, most or all of us have learned that preparation can be very important, such as gathering receipts for a tax accountant or completing a driver's education course before obtaining a license. Some of those seasons occur naturally, like the nine months of pregnancy which allow us time to prepare for bringing a child into this world. And there are intentional seasons of preparation, like an athlete who trains for months and years ahead of the Olympic Games. No matter how it happens, the end result is hopefully "a state of readiness." We become ready to do what we need to do, give what we need to give, and receive what we need to receive. I have tried, more times than I care to remember, to jump into significant situations *without* sufficient preparation. It often led to failure and heartache. But when we "seek a state of readiness"—and do it with God's help—He gives us clearer vision, accurate hearing, abundant strength, and the active motivation to follow through to the end. In other words: God prepares us to succeed. So, I find it interesting that, before we get to Step Seven where we humbly ask God to remove our shortcomings, Step Six talks about *being ready* to have them removed. It is the Principle of Preparation.

Before moving ahead, let me review the first five Steps by offering a paraphrase of each:

Step 1: Admitted that we have certain addictions, weaknesses, habits, feelings, circumstances, and/or relationships that we cannot fix on our own and that *trying* to fix them on our own makes us feel crazy.

Step 2: Made the choice to believe that there is a Greater Power who loves us and wants to work in our lives and help us to *not* feel crazy. We call Him God.

Step 3: Made the logical decision to daily submit our wills and our lives to the care of this Greater Power, trusting that He will open up new pathways to freedom.

Step 4: Asked God to help us identify and deal with any deficits, or defects of character, that are keeping us from *finding* that pathway to freedom.

Step 5: Talked to God, ourselves, and another human being, about the deficits or defects we are discovering.

Which brings us to Step Six, which says: **Were entirely ready to have God remove all these defects of character.**[23]

So, you may be asking: What are defects of character?

I think of them as old ways of dealing with life that don't work. In Alcoholics Anonymous meetings, there is often a list of these defects posted on a wall. It's not an exhaustive list, but it represents a fair number of character traits that interfere with healthy living and are often a catalyst for addictive behaviors, such as anger, anxiety, dishonesty, pride, guilt, jealousy, perfectionism, revenge, and self-seeking. Those are less-than-desirable traits that most or all people deal with at some point and in some way, but addicts have a tendency to take things to a different level. We don't do things halfway. We go for the gusto.

The common thread that runs through the list of character defects is that they block peace of mind and disrupt relationships, whether with other people, with God, and/or with ourselves. And in my mind, they keep us in a place of distrust. They are coping mechanisms used especially when life feels out of control. Over time, it has become abundantly clear to me that God's desire for us is to operate from a position of reliance upon Him.

... Every day and in every circumstance.

This is discipleship. This is how Jesus lived during His time on earth and how He still lives now—in consistent, continual dependence upon God. This is what works for us, too: abiding under the shadow of His wings, making Him our refuge and our fortress, not relying on our own insight or understanding, but placing our trust in Him with all of our hearts. This is the true place of strength and peace.

However, when you don't know how to trust, character defects may become the default mode. They may be all you have in the moment. Most folks who become addicted are already functioning from a position of lack—something essential got left out. Maybe it was love, affirmation, emotional support, or something as basic as food and shelter. This lack creates pain and leaves you feeling incomplete, inadequate, and inferior.

Those exact words describe the beliefs that I held about myself for many years, and I often wondered why I felt that way. But one day I had a "moving picture" roll through my mind that perfectly visualized the malady. It was just like an image being projected onto a screen; like a silent film from the 1920s:

I saw myself as a child, being put together on an assembly line at a "human factory." But while I was going down the conveyor belt, several workers weren't paying attention, and they overlooked the fact that I didn't get all my parts—not the physical parts—but the emotional parts that go on the inside.

Someone had made a horrible mistake! I begged them, with lots of beseeching facial expressions and flailing arms, to let me go through the line again and get it right this time. But no one was paying attention, and I couldn't seem to speak actual words. When I got to the end of the conveyor belt, I fell onto a steep, slippery slide that took me for a fast ride and propelled me out the back door of the factory without so much as a "by your leave." And then the door slammed shut behind me with a resounding thud that kept echoing in my mind. I knew I had just been thrown into life ... as an incomplete human being.

I felt absolutely terrified.

Stop the film.

Lack creates fear, which very often becomes the root cause of addiction. To simplify, addiction is usually a temporary painkiller, a cover-up for fear, and a very poor substitute for healthy living and happy relationships. Fear, itself, is a character defect, but I also believe that it helps to create other character flaws, all of which collectively become our tools for dealing with life, however unsuccessfully.

In spite of that fact, being ready to have God remove our defects of character can still be a challenge. God knows that we have a natural resistance to change, so He gives us time to work through that issue. Change is scary. Ordinarily, at least for a certain period of time, we want the status quo, even when the status quo stinks. We want things to stay the same, even if they're stagnating. We want what's familiar, even when we start realizing that what's familiar is destructive. That's certainly how it was working for me. Ironically, I thought if things stayed the same, I would be safe. But that was a subconscious delusion—a deception, a falsehood, and a lie. And even when it became abundantly clear that something needed to change, I didn't know how to approach the task in a way that worked.

This is how it usually went: I would work really hard at trying to keep things the same until some part of my damaged heart would realize that keeping things the same was essentially killing me. Then I would purposely (and I thought, valiantly) throw myself into a scenario of big, dramatic change. But the big, dramatic changes created fear and anxiety that swallowed me up like a tornadic wind and held me in a vise-like grip until I relented. Then I ran as fast as I could back to the land where all was familiar again ... but still killing me. I don't know about you, but that sounds like insanity to me. And it sure felt insane.

Here's a classic example: in 1994, the church my husband and I were pastoring, as well as our marriage, were in the midst of a downward spiral that eventually led to the final demise of both. All of it was complicated, out of control, and completely overwhelming. Since I wasn't very good at trusting God at the time, I decided that I needed to step away from full-time ministry and get a secular job. I'm sure I was "running away," but in my mind, it seemed logical. And needful. After the usual job-hunting procedure, I landed a position at a local bank, and they scheduled me for training. This was big, big dramatic change for me on every level, and I had been dealing with tons of anxiety from the start of the process. But, instead of seeing that as a red flag, I kept moving forward because anxiety was just a part of daily living for me; it was highly uncomfortable but "normal."

On the first day of training, being one of several new employees, I suddenly started having a panic attack. It's hard to describe a panic attack if you've never had one. But if you have, you'll know what I'm talking about. As I was sitting there watching a teaching video, minding my own business, my brain began to "freeze up." I could not comprehend the simplest concept that was being presented. I couldn't even take notes, which ordinarily was an easy task. A sensation of creeping fear began in the small of my back and slowly moved up my spine toward my neck and over the top of my head. It felt like a shroud. A suffocating blanket. And it just kept wrapping around me tighter and tighter to where I could barely breathe.

When I was sure I couldn't sit there any longer, trying to pretend that all was well, the trainer thankfully gave us a short break. I was so desperate to get out of there and make the panic stop that I went into a room across the hall and faked a phone call to a fictitious third party. After hanging up from the fictitious call, I proceeded to tell my bank trainer that I had just received a more lucrative job offer and had decided to take it. Needless to say, she was very unhappy with me. I didn't care. I gathered my belongings and shot out of there like the building was on fire. I had never experienced anything like it before, nor do I ever want to experience it again. I've had mild panic attacks since then, but nothing like that one.

So, what did I do? I drove straight to the grocery store, purchased a giant bag of binge food, and hit a fast-food restaurant on my way home. The afternoon was spent in oblivion. I was unequivocally mortified by the choices I had made during the bank training that day, and the panic attack was so unnerving that I almost had a panic attack thinking about having another panic attack. It felt like something outside of myself took me over, manipulating me into doing something that was strange, immoral, and out of character. I didn't know where it had come from. That was one of those times when I had the sensation of stepping out of my body as I watched someone else do what I did. The shame moved in like a tsunami.

And I didn't know how to fix it.

Within a few days, I made arrangements for my kids and me to go home to Kansas to visit my parents. We stayed for a month. I was literally trying to run away from my situation and myself, and I knew it. But when the kids and I traveled back to Maryland, I just picked up where I left off. I went back to what I had been doing for eleven years, even though all the problems were still in place and no resolutions had been found. The fear in my life was so strong that I simply wanted to stick with what was familiar, even though I knew in my heart that it wasn't working. I really just wanted someone to wake me up from the nightmare, so I could be done with it.

But it wasn't a dream.

That experience was indicative of how crazy life could be in the midst of addiction and dysfunction. Take some challenging circumstances, add a long list of character defects, and what you end up with is a mess. I knew something was wrong with me, and I knew I had character defects. But I didn't know how to eradicate them from my life. Many years later, when I had commenced upon the Twelve Step journey, I took a good look at Step Six and realized that the simple truth is this: in order to have the kind of life I want, I have to be willing to deal with my character defects ... by letting God deal with them. The deficits have to go, or at least they have to start getting better.

But the problem was, on some level, I had been trying to remove these character defects for years without reaching the goal. What was going to be different this time? Well, the main difference was that, this time, the Defect-Remover was God. Part of Step Six is a clear knowledge of who has the power. I knew I would never be ready to deal with these deficits if I was relying on my own strength. Dependence on God's strength was one big component that prepared me to move forward.

In the Old Testament, the Lord told Joshua, "Do not be afraid or discouraged. For the Lord your God is with you wherever you go" (Joshua 1:9, NLT). I see three truths in that scripture: 1) God is all powerful; 2) He is with me; and 3) I belong to Him. God obligates Himself to sustain, protect, and assist those who belong to Him. It's part of our covenant; it's a two-way contract. I turn my life over to God, and He takes care of me.

And God knows how to take care of His kids.

I once had the accelerator on my car suddenly stick while I was driving in heavy, rush-hour traffic in Ft. Worth, Texas. It didn't just stick; the car accelerated without my foot being on the pedal. Talk about unnerving. What stopped the vehicle was a sideways skid into a speed zone sign as the car was swerving out of control. We were going so fast at the time of impact that the sign was imbedded seven inches into the metal frame of that car: a 1969 Delta '88 Oldsmobile. A tank. The unusual thing is: my son and I didn't move one single inch when we rammed into that iron signpost. It was like we were cushioned in a soft cloud.

However, after the accident, I had difficulty getting into that car to drive anywhere. The fear of a reoccurrence was very strong because the garage repairman couldn't find anything wrong with the vehicle. As I prayed about it, God told me to close my eyes and "relive" the accident in my mind—but to take Jesus with me this time. I could see Jesus sitting in the middle of the front seat—one of those old bench seats—with His left arm around me on the driver's side, and His right arm around my two-year old son on the passenger side. At the time of impact, all three of us were supernaturally held in place. We didn't feel a thing.

Now, all I know to tell you is that visualizing the accident with Jesus sitting between us and protecting us totally vaporized the fear. God was with us. I drove that car for another year before we sold it. I have concluded that when God says He will be with us, we need to understand that He's not just saying nice, sweet words to help us feel better. He means it. It's a promise that carries supernatural power. It's a force. And sometimes an unexplainable force.

So, to apply that truth:

With God at my side, I have all the assistance I need, and I hold the belief that He is with me all the time. This provides a solid sense of safety and security that forms a launchpad for forward movement—movement that creates the much-desired progress. These days, when I see that a character defect needs to be removed, my approach is very different. For one thing, change has become a frequent part of my journey, and sometimes, I actually look forward to the change and there's no anxiety involved. Other times, there is. In which case, I let God help me deal with the fear of change before I ever get to the actual change. Sometimes, just sitting down to talk with a trusted friend is enough to break through the anxiety. Sometimes He takes away the fear once I see it for what it is, and sometimes He gives me the courage to choose change, even when I'm still afraid. Sometimes you just have to look fear in the face and tell it to go back where it came from. With gusto.

Ultimately, Step Six is about trusting that the release of things which are familiar, but useless, leads to a much better pathway with God as the Guide. It's about discovering healthier ways to cope and navigate through life, believing that I can feel good about myself as new choices are being made. Can I let go of the old and usher in the new? Can I trust God to be there? Can I deal with the unfamiliar long enough to give it a chance to produce good results? Those are all questions that I have asked myself in one way or another. And when the answers to the questions are yes, I have more opportunities to watch the Lord working in my life in powerful ways.

Choosing to walk in faith has rewards.

One more thought before the wrap up: A season of preparing for the removal of character defects always includes opening yourself to new ways of thinking and feeling. If I try to change what I'm doing without first changing what I'm thinking ... it doesn't usually work very well.

New thoughts = New feelings = New choices.

This is part of God's design for change, and He abundantly provides what we need through His Word and through the Twelve Step program. He creates a vision for the new, which comes into focus as we study real-life characters in His Word and as we hear the testimonies of others in Twelve Step meetings. Those two resources are invaluable; they inspire and generate heart-faith. It gives me hope to look at Peter, who went from being an impulsive, hotheaded fisherman, to being a consistent, steady, and highly influential apostle of the church. If he can change, so can I. Jesus didn't just wave a magic wand, and suddenly the fiery disciple was a different man. I believe Peter had to work at it with God's help, just like I do. And Twelve Step meetings are full of people who have been miraculously transformed. All you have to do is listen. God uses the experience, strength, and hope of others to mentally, emotionally, and visually prepare me for success—which never ceases to amaze me. It's brilliant.

But in light of all that I've shared, I have to be honest and say that there isn't a by-the-book process that automatically prepares us for working the Twelve Steps. If you go to Twelve Step meetings, you'll hear someone say, "You're ready when you're ready, and not before." And it's true. God is the only one who really knows what will help us in this endeavor. So, I encourage people to pray and ask God for that specific help. He knows exactly who and what to bring into our lives to create the perfect state of preparedness, and He's happy to answer that prayer if we will be brave enough to pray. It's a classic example of the fact that this is a very spiritual Program that leads us to faith as we choose to walk in faith.

Truthfully, Step Six is one more Step that brings me face-to-face with The Gift. Recovery, for me, is about finally seeing the true character and nature of God, and I really love what I'm seeing. In my whole life, I've never loved God as much as I do now. He has delighted Himself in showing me His faithfulness and the genuine depth of His love for me. There were so many things I realize I didn't have, or didn't receive, because I never asked for them with any kind of sincere faith. I was often so full of fear that I didn't bother to ask God for much of anything at all. But, personally, the most magnificent benefit of this Program is God Himself. He has given Himself to everyone as a gift. He gives Himself to me as a gift.

It's just that this time ... I took off the bow and opened up the package.

Even in that, He knew there was a season of preparation, and He orchestrated it beautifully.

Step Seven:
I Can't ... But He Can

LIVING IN KANSAS, I'm no stranger to inclement weather.

We can have thunderstorms roll through with torrential rain, seventy-mile-per-hour winds, and golf ball-sized hail. If your vehicle gets caught out in the thick of it, you can count on sustaining damage. Unfortunately, sometimes the hail damage is enough to total the vehicle, but at other times, it can be repaired. Thankfully, there are people who go through specialized training to learn how to "remove" the dents and make the car look as good as new, which can be a lucrative business in this state.

In like fashion, Step Seven can be a bit like "dent removal." It says: *Humbly asked Him to remove our shortcomings.*[24] It's not too much of a stretch to see my defects and shortcomings as damage that needs to be repaired, which then puts God in the position of "Dent Remover." (Now *that's* job security.) In the beginning, I wasn't quite sure how all of this was supposed to work, but there was no question that my defects needed to be addressed. The further I went in recovery, the more I realized that shortcomings feed into addictive tendencies, like heat and humidity feed into a thunderstorm. And my shortcomings were creating big "thunderstorms."

So, I'm very thankful that God is more than able to accomplish this work in my life and that He never looked at me as a Lost Cause. *I* sometimes did, but He didn't. There have been many occasions when God revealed that *He just wasn't going to give up on me.* Even when I fully expected Him to and wouldn't have blamed Him at all if He had. More than once, realizing the depth of His mercy and faithfulness, I have sat and sobbed like a baby, as my despair changed to relief. I knew if He gave up on me, I was done. I could just throw in the towel and make my exit.

"Hasta la vista, baby."

But I discovered that God specializes in healing and wholeness. He loves it. When I read the Gospels, I see Jesus traveling all over the place dispensing this "specialty" everywhere He goes—healing blind men and lepers, delivering demoniacs and tormented souls, and releasing adulterous women and greedy tax collectors from the captivity of sin. He said He was here to show us the Father. "Anyone who has seen Me has seen the Father!" (John 14:9b, NLT) So, instead of us drowning in shame and hopelessness, God throws out a lifeline of grace and mercy and says, "I want to heal you. I want to deliver you. I want you to be free from that which holds you captive."

The Heart of God is an awesome thing to behold.

But for a long time, my inner belief was that God only helped people who were obedient and mostly perfect. He sure wasn't going to help anyone as weak and rebellious and sinful as me. In that regard, Step Seven did present a difficulty. I had no problem admitting that I had lots of shortcomings, or character defects, but asking God to remove them was about as familiar to me as the eating habits of an aardvark. So, in the Twelve Step program, I began by choosing to believe that God was totally willing to do for me what I could not do for myself. That became a viable choice substantiated by the stories of others in support group meetings who had experienced miraculous recovery through the power of a loving God. Those stories caused faith to rise up in me like the flood waters of the Mississippi River. It overflowed the banks of my unbelief, and a new wave of genuine trust began to fill my soul.

The other element that was initially confusing was the concept of humility because Step Seven says to make the request humbly. I used to be completely embarrassed by my imperfections, and certainly had tried to get rid of the ones of which I was aware. But my repeated failures only led to more embarrassment. So, when Step Seven instructed me to "humbly" ask God to remove my shortcomings, I needed some clarification. I was less familiar with humility and more familiar with humiliation. I didn't need any more of that. But I have come to understand that those two things are very different. Humiliation is basically having embarrassment and shame dumped on your head. But humility means that I'm in a posture of surrender when I make a request—ready and willing to allow God to do whatever He wants because I trust Him. He's the Potter, I'm the clay. Part of humility is being willing to ask for help. Part of it is choosing to let go of pride. Part of it is being willing to change. And part of it is depending on God to provide the power to change. None of that is easy, but it's completely doable. And what I've noticed about humble people is that they often seem to embrace contentment and simplicity and are at peace with themselves and others.

That's good stuff.

Make no mistake, however, this Step requires two-way involvement. I was sitting in a Twelve Step study recently, and one person in attendance that night asked a great question. She wanted to know how to actively participate in the process of change—that surely God wasn't supposed to do all the work. And she's right. Although He occasionally throws out an overnight, miraculous cure, the answer is usually mutual effort and joint cooperation ... mine and God's. I used to have a terrible problem with social anxiety, and it often kept me at home or cowering in the corner in a group setting. But, as an example of mutual effort, I chose to step out and "make" myself attend a social event, and God's part was to help me be comfortable around the people who were there. I literally learned to "pray and go." God can't give me social ease if I'm not interacting with others. So, oftentimes, a character defect is changed by choosing to do the opposite of what you used to do, utilizing the assistance that God offers. If you do that frequently enough, recognizing that it begins as an act of faith, it will create the desired result.

"... faith is dead without good works" (James 2:26, NLT). You have to add actions to your beliefs.

So, let me bring this closer to home with some applications involving my own, personal character defects. My biggest, most glaring defect has been Fear. I have learned in recovery that large portions of my life were influenced, and even consumed, by fear. Almost every major area has been tainted by this unseemly force ... and I call it a "force" because there are times it appears to have a life of its own. It would take multiple pages to cover all the ways that fear has held me by its tentacles.

In AA's *Twelve Steps and Twelve Traditions*, it states that "the chief activator of our defects has been self-centered fear—primarily fear that we would lose something we already possessed or would fail to get something we demanded."[25]

When I first read that, I reluctantly, but fully agreed, and in hindsight, realized that every negative, life-damaging decision I ever made was based on some kind of fear. That revelation cut me to the quick. I have always wanted to be brave and courageous. I wanted to be the sort of person who could face anything in life with an affirming, resolute trust. And I was far from it. On the other hand, every positive, life-enhancing decision I ever made was based on faith. The two could not be any more opposite, and seeing them in juxtaposition helps me to realize how Step Seven works: since fear is the "chief activator" of character defects, then the solution lies in the realm of faith and trust.

In light of that, my "Seventh Steps" often include a request for God to remove fear in my heart and to heal the root source of that fear. It also includes a concurrent prayer asking Him to increase my faith and trust. The great thing is that I'm actually seeing answers to these prayers. It may not be an instant result, or even an overnight result, but rather a gradual change that becomes noticeable over time. Here's just one example: I took a job a few years ago that unexpectedly had one big challenge after another. Since it was a new position, I expected a learning curve, but this went beyond that. The anxiety was overwhelming, and panic lurked around the corner. But, with frequent petitions to God, I was progressively able to face each difficulty and handle it successfully. My fear changed to faith. In those repeated victories, I learned to not only place my confidence in Him but to also place an appropriate amount of confidence in myself. Something which was lacking at the time. This was no small thing for me, and it was a catalyst for important growth.

A second, closely related shortcoming that used to follow me like the plague was letting my emotions control me, especially if the emotion was rejection. In the past when rejection hit, it was immediately followed by the reinforcement of three "old tapes" which loudly declared: "I'm not loved," "Nothing I do is good enough," and "If someone really gets to know me, they won't like me." Those were very codependent, and fearful, beliefs that I had carried around my whole life. And if I let those thoughts take hold, they would quickly lead to anger, hopelessness, and/or self-pity. It's my party, and I'll cry if I want to ... right? It's easy to see how these shortcomings can multiply and snowball.

My response is much saner, now. I'm able to step back and look at the person or situation from a more realistic perspective accompanied by more realistic reasoning. Most of the time, I can simply choose to not feel rejected and let it go. The sense of rejection doesn't grab hold of me like it used to, controlling my thoughts and reactions. Sometimes I have to work on it for a while and ask God for some assistance. But when I sense a more level-headed response kicking into gear, I don't take it for granted. I'm very grateful to God for the kind of growth that empowers me to live in a place of serenity.

A third character defect I have to mention is running away from problems—the cut-and-run syndrome. This, unfortunately, has been a big one as well. Looking back, I think it started with the abortion, where I "ran away" from the overwhelming challenge of raising a child instead of facing up to the responsibility. Then I "ran away" from the shame and guilt I was feeling by breaking up with Danny (which didn't work). I ran away from Maryland when the pain of a church split and a failing marriage became too much for me to handle. I have "run away" from all kinds of negativity—like boredom, frustration, or unresolved conflict—by eating, reading, or watching television. I have even tried to run away from problems with the "geographical cure," where you actually move, or change your geographical location, in the belief that said move will make the chaos and turmoil on the inside of you magically disappear. It doesn't. Running away doesn't change what's on the inside, but the delusion of escape can become a mental "fix" that relieves the pressure, at least for a while.

In the past, one of my favorite ways to run away was to think about living in a luxurious home overlooking a beautiful lake. I would get on the Internet and spend time looking at expensive homes surrounded by water and tall, majestic trees. There's no question that it was soothing, and very diverting, to daydream about drinking coffee on the deck while watching geese feed down by the water. I could mentally go to that place and actually alter my mood until it was time to get off the computer and face reality again. What I actually needed, all along, was to let God help me address a general state of inner discontent (another character defect). There are forms of escape that all "normal" people use, like occasionally watching a movie to take a break from stress. But the negative difference for me was purposefully trying to change my mood through the escape. Repetition of that scenario became addictive.

You can see how I've given my "Dent Remover" a lot of job security.

It's a good thing He's up to the task.

It's also a good thing that He isn't looking for perfection. In recovery, we learn that God is happy with progress.

Now, sometimes a shortcoming is not something we did but something that happened to us, and through that event, a message was perceived and internalized. The message itself can then become a defect that hinders and negatively influences our lives. Once again, God's answer is to bring healing.

When I was in elementary school, my granddaddy owned a motel on Tenth Street, and he gave us permission to swim in its modest little pool anytime we wanted. We often had it all to ourselves, so it was almost like having our own pool, except that we had to drive a couple of miles to get there. For several summers in a row, Mom took all of us kids there once or twice a week. It would be sunny and hot, and I can still picture the bright blue sky looming overhead as I floated faceup in the water on my back. The white clouds would move across the open expanse like a slow wagon train, making me smile with fantasies of being a pioneer girl traveling across the prairie.

We would jump off the small diving board, splash around in the shallow end, and dive for rocks on the bottom of the pool. There were also competitions to see who could swim the farthest under water and long sessions of playing catch with plastic balls or anything else that would float and was convenient to throw. After swimming for a while, we would carefully lay our towels out on the hot cement and soak up the warmth of the sun until our skin was dry and politely scorched by the strong heat. Then we would jump back into the water and start all over again. A trip to Granddaddy's pool was often the highlight of the week. All good memories, except for one.

In July of 1961, three months before my seventh birthday, Dad took us to swim for a couple of hours on a Saturday afternoon. My older brother and sister were diving for rocks in the shallow end, Dad had my two-year-old brother seated in a lounge chair close to him, and I was dog-paddling around in the deep end. I hadn't taken swimming lessons yet, so dog-paddling was the extent of my water skills. Dad was talking with someone who had stopped by, and he must have become distracted because my little brother crawled out of the chair and out onto the diving board without Dad noticing. I paddled underneath the end of the board, thinking it would be great fun to play with him in the water, and told him to jump on in. What I didn't realize, with my six-year-old intellect, was that my brother didn't know how to dog-paddle.

He jumped in.

Or more like ... he let himself fall off the end of the board into my arms. I caught him and was really surprised at how heavy he was—and was then equally surprised that he didn't start paddling around. I got my arms underneath him to try to keep him from going under and kicked with my feet as hard as I could. But in trying to lift him up to keep his head above water, I ended up inadvertently pushing myself under. Struggling to the surface three different times, I tried to call for help, but there was only time to gasp for air. I was tiring quickly, and the weight of a two-year-old was too much for my six-year-old strength. We couldn't have been in the water for more than forty-five seconds, if that long, but it felt like an eternity. And when I went under after that third gasping breath, I still had hold of my brother ... but I knew I wasn't coming up again.

Just at that moment, I felt the weight of his body being lifted off. My arms were free. I came to the surface and struggled over to the edge of the pool to catch my breath, amazed at how sweet the air felt in my lungs. Looking up, I saw my father crawl out of the pool with his two-year old son and move toward a towel to get him dried off and settled down. Dad looked at me to make sure I was alright and was visibly relieved to see that I was, but he didn't say anything. So, once I was rested, and not knowing what else to do, I joined my other siblings in a game of catch.

But that, unfortunately, was not the end of the episode.

The problem was, I had almost drowned, and my six-year-old brain recognized how close I had come to dying. My dad, however, didn't know what I was thinking or what I had just experienced. It seemed a little strange to me that he didn't say anything after he pulled my little brother out. But I figured he would tell Mom when we got home, and they would both talk to me that evening. Actually, I wondered if I would be in big, bad trouble since I was the one who encouraged my sibling to jump in.

But there was no talk.

Mom said nothing. Dad said nothing. No one mentioned the incident in any way, shape, or form. At that point in my life, on some level, I interpreted that silence as indifference. Like, no one cared whether I lived or died. Somehow, that day, an unspoken message began to take hold. It played quietly like a broken record in the back of my mind, but I couldn't quite make out the words. They were there, but slightly out of an understandable hearing range. I just knew they were bad, and I didn't want to think about it.

Along with that vague message came feelings of sadness and fear that were sometimes suffocating, just like the experience in the pool. I didn't know exactly what to call it back then, but I knew that it felt heavy, and I couldn't make it go away. Unconsciously, very negative thoughts about myself began to settle into the core of my being. And even though the beliefs weren't actually true at the time, they were conclusions based on my young perceptions.

... Perceptions which became my reality.

After that, I can remember my initial experiences with depression. I sometimes went outside to swing on the swing set and would pump back and forth with rhythmic motions for an hour at a time. It was soothing. It helped. It made me feel not so alone. There was something inherently peaceful about watching the sky and listening to the birds sing as I floated up closer to the trees. That was also the same summer that I started eating a lot of sugar bread. I must have done it before, but probably not four pieces at once.

Forty-four years passed before I fully realized the message that had been internalized with that whole event. The message was: my existence didn't matter. And, in many respects, I lived decades of my life based on that foundational belief. But all those years later, God also gave me the opportunity to learn the truth. I got to hear Dad's version of that story, and as I listened, it dawned on me for the first time that Someone who was very good had saved my life that July afternoon—and the life of my little brother as well. Having been invited over for Easter dinner, and since God had just revealed to me the "message" of the near-drowning, I decided to ask Dad about the incident. I wasn't sure if he would remember anything at all. He was eighty years old at the time, and several years into alcoholic dementia, but his long-term memory was still good. His eyes got big at the recollection of the event, and he went on to share that he had been chatting with an acquaintance over by the fence. With the distraction, his back was turned to the pool, and he had assumed that my little brother was still lounging in a chair close by.

The next thing he knew, he heard a voice telling him to, "Get those kids out of the water NOW!"

He said it wasn't an audible voice—just words that he heard on the inside—but the urgency was very clear. He turned around and looked over at the deep end of the pool where I was struggling underwater with my little brother on top of me. So, Dad jumped in, grabbed my brother, and climbed out. He said he realized on some level that it had been a very dangerous situation, and he said it "scared him to death." But when he assessed my condition afterward, I appeared to be okay, so he didn't say anything more to me about it. And he didn't mention it to Mom. Mom never knew.

Dad had no idea that I had almost drowned that day. He thought I was fine. I was fine, physically. But mentally and emotionally, my six-year-old life had just dramatically changed.

I share that to make a specific point: we can be strongly and subconsciously influenced by "messages" in our lives, and it's worth a certain amount of investigation to discover and resolve any underlying themes. The goal is wholeness that leads to strength, contentment, productivity, and peace. This is God's will for us. So, in my Seventh Step work, I have learned to ask God to show me any messages that are still creating negative outcomes. He has been faithful to do that. He was the one who revealed the "drowning message" to me in the first place. He knew I was ready to deal with it, and change it, because I had the tools to do so by that time. What "healed" that message was finding out that God had been there supernaturally protecting me all through the event. And, obviously, my existence mattered to someone. Not only did it matter to my parents, but also to the Creator of the Universe, my Heavenly Father. The Truth is the truth, and it still sets us free.

As for the negative message I carried for decades, I have accepted it as part of my journey. And it brings to light the fact that we are better able to show compassion and give comfort to those who are experiencing the same sufferings we have already endured. There are millions of people all around the world who still carry the message that their "existence doesn't matter." Whenever and wherever I meet them, by God's divine orchestration, I will know the pain in their hearts as others cannot. We will have irrefutable common ground that forms an instant bond between us, and I will be able to offer the same comfort and hope to them that God has given to me (2 Corinthians 1:4–6, NLT).

I count that a privilege.

In the end, all of the Twelve Steps, especially Step Seven, are designed to help me effectively deal with my shortcomings, as well as their root sources. I tried for years to get the job done myself—and couldn't.

But He can.

And honestly, the simple goal of Step Seven is just to become a better person. That's a reasonable and logical goal since I began my recovery in a state of self-hatred. Liking who I am, being loved by God, and being accepted by others goes a long way toward having a happy, useful life. That's what most of us want in the first place. So, I have determined to work Step Seven every time I need to. And since God promises that we are "constantly being transformed into His very own image ... from one degree of glory to another" (2 Corinthians 3:18, AMPC), I'm expecting awesome results.

Step Eight:
Not for the Faint of Heart

WHEN I WAS TWENTY YEARS OLD and experiencing episodes of clinical depression, it felt like I was losing my mind. And maybe I was. All I know is that I felt quietly and secretly terrified because I never knew whether or not I would one day have an episode that never ended. The thought made my toes curl up in fear and dread. Up until then, the depression would last three to four days, and then something would help me temporarily snap out of it. I could never figure out how each episode started or stopped, and there was the definite sensation of being manipulated by a mad scientist with wild, unruly hair and squinty, evil eyes.

So, in the midst of that torment, the one very clear desire on the inside of me was to feel peace ... to have freedom from agitating thoughts, oppressive emotions, and the darkness of my soul. That's what led me to Jesus. And truthfully, He brought a light into my life that released me from that heavy oppression. Since then, I have definitely struggled, but not with that same level of despair that consumed me before.

1 Peter 3 tells us, "... search for peace (harmony; undisturbedness from fears, agitating passions, and moral conflicts) and seek it eagerly. [Do not merely desire peaceful relations with God, with your fellowmen, and with yourself, but pursue, and go after them]" (1 Peter 3:11, AMPC).

Peace is evidently no small thing in the sight of God, and that's one big reason why recovery is important to Him. Working the Steps and principles *leads* me to that peace, and that prime objective was the locomotive engine behind my commitment to Step Eight. This is another Step where strong motivation is necessary because it says: ***Made of list of all persons we had harmed, and became willing to make amends to them all.***[26]

Wow.

Whoever said "working the Twelve Steps is *not* for sissies" ... knew what they were talking about.

My first experience with Steps Eight and Nine came long before I ever actually heard the verbiage. A year after I became a Christian, at the age of twenty-one, I was encouraged by a mentor to pray and ask God for the names of five people I had hurt in my past and ask them to forgive me. This was presented to me as a means of resolving relationship issues, so I wouldn't carry that "baggage" further into my walk with the Lord. It was explained that offenses (no matter which end you're on) often become a mental, emotional, and spiritual hindrance.

And sometimes a huge stumbling block. That made sense to me, and I very much wanted to have peace with God and with others, so I agreed to the task. I really thought it might take *longer* than thirty seconds for God to give me those five names ... but ... it didn't.

After fervently praying for the Lord to give me courage, I approached each person on my list and asked forgiveness from them all. I did this either face-to-face or through written correspondence, depending on the situation and where they lived. A hundred pounds lifted off of me when the amends were complete, and because of that positive result, I have purposed to continue this practice in my Christian life over the last several decades. There have been times when I was slow to recognize the need to make amends, but God has always been faithful to bring it to my attention sooner or later.

Few people want to take responsibility and admit their faults, and since I'm one of them, it's a good thing that I learned to ask God for honesty, openness, and willingness. Otherwise, I would have been up the proverbial creek without a paddle. There are many, many ways that I have caused harm to people in my life: I have been selfish, self-focused, and overly dependent in my codependency; neglectful of my spouse and children in acting out my bingeing addiction; domineering in my need to be in control; angry in my defensiveness; full of self-pity in my pain; verbally abusive in retaliation; emotionally abusive in putting up walls to protect myself; physically abusive to my own body, which is God's temple; and hurtful toward God in choosing idols in place of Him.

In many of those earlier situations, however, I was blind to my offenses. Sometimes I was just very self-focused, or I saw myself as the *victim*. Victims are innocent by definition. Victims aren't the wrongdoers. The perpetrators are the ones doing the harm; victims are the recipients of that harm. But over time, I began to see *my part* and the harm that I was doing or had done. Sometimes, we are victims and perpetrators at the same time. A classic example was when I got pregnant the summer after I graduated from high school. I was so focused on the predicament and my own pain that I was oblivious to what was going on with my boyfriend. He wanted to get married because he actually loved me. But, although I agreed at first, a multitude of fears finally helped me give in to the suggestion of an abortion. And, it mortifies me to admit that I didn't want my whole life to change because of a baby. My boyfriend had no say in the matter.

Four years later, after I became a Christian, he was the first person on my amends list. I clearly saw how selfish and unfair I had been with him—not to mention what I did to the baby. I had to ask our baby to forgive me, too. God helped me do that through prayer and counseling. And, even though it took thirty-five years, my former boyfriend and I finally had the opportunity to talk about that traumatic time in our lives. In fact, over a long period, we had good and honest email discussions about all the major aspects of the situation—not every day, but as memories and issues came to the surface. It didn't take too long to see that a "Divine Third Party" was involved with our process, and I will always be very grateful for the chance to deal with that situation head-on. The damage was deep, and in our own individual ways, we were being held captive. So, the healing has not only been beneficial, but it has also been life changing. We each had perceptions to correct, forgiveness to give and receive, grief to share, and joyful memories to appreciate. What was once a huge, negative turning point in my life became an immeasurable blessing. And the lessons learned about relationships, choices, love, fear, compassion, selfishness, passivity, and grace have been irreplaceable. For Danny and me, the end result was *release* ... with wings to fly.

I will never question God's ability to resolve trauma.

It's also impossible to overlook the incredible mercy of the Lord in this set of circumstances. Frankly, everyone involved made mistakes, but when I think about what I did to our child, to Danny, to all four of our parents, and to myself—no extension of mercy was deserved. Nonetheless, mercy was given. And that was the redeeming power of God at work in the midst of fallen humanity.

But God didn't stop there.

When Danny and I were going together back in high school, my family was in the midst of utter turmoil, and I was a mess. But I felt completely loved and accepted by Danny's mom and dad, as well as his sister. They opened their arms to me, providing a respite and refuge at a time when I felt like I was drowning alone in a sea of despair. In actuality, I have wondered if God was trying to give me exactly what I needed: unconditional love. I was especially close to Danny's dad. He was so very much like the father I had always wanted: kind, protective, affectionate, caring, fun, and easy to talk to. I found myself wanting to divulge my heartaches to him and gained the benefit of his wisdom when I did so on an occasion or two.

That summer after high school graduation, when I found out I was pregnant, I even had a chance to officially become one of their family members. Because Danny wanted marriage between us, he went to great lengths to show his willingness to begin to provide for me and the baby in my womb. He secured a full-time job and found a house for us to rent—a little white house with shade trees in the front yard and everything we needed. He would have taken on the responsibility with an open heart, but I was terrified, and in the end ... I played the "escape artist" in more ways than one.

Danny and I had *lots* to talk about thirty-five years later.

As for his father, he and I had the chance to reconnect at my dad's funeral service in 2007. We had coffee soon thereafter, caught up on life, and eventually realized that we had adopted each other long ago as "father and daughter." It was a love that had passed the test of time, distance, silence, and a lack of opportunity. And in reuniting, especially after the death of his first wife and the passing of my dad, we found a treasure in our relationship with each other. A great joy. To this day, we still keep in touch and live close enough to see each other on a fairly frequent basis. We never part company without a hug and an "I love you."

Now, how do you fathom a God like that?

It's beyond my comprehension.

Another example of facing my role as a perpetrator involved my relationship with my first husband. There's no question that he hurt me and was emotionally abusive in our relationship. But it took me a lot longer to step out of my victim role and see how *my* words and actions had been hurtful and abusive toward *him*. As is usually the case, I was not able to see and *own* much of my personal responsibility until *after* the divorce, at which point I wrote a letter to him asking his forgiveness and reciting to him that which I had done wrong. Over a period of years, as more things came to light in my recovery, I wrote three different letters to him. Unfortunately, he has not responded, but my peace comes from knowing that I have done what God asked me to do.

Step Eight is largely about facing the truth that people who are hurting inside have a tendency to bring pain to others.[27] But because we are so often blind to our own offenses, it can take a little longer to see how we purposely or inadvertently caused harm, even when there was no intention of doing so. I was no exception. I was much too focused on how other people were hurting *me*.

But Step Eight takes you down a different road.

When I made my first list of names, while in active recovery, all of the names came from my inventory. At the time, my self-examination had the propensity to create shame and fear, so, I found myself wanting to point fingers. My defense strategy was to come up with all the reasons why *their* offenses were every bit as bad as *mine*. After all, conflicts are rarely one-sided; it usually takes two imperfect people making human mistakes. But looking at someone else's fault is not what this Step is about. As with the other Steps and principles, God is looking for my humility, my obedience, and my willingness. Those three things are about character development, and I'm learning that God is *all over* character development. He knows, much better than I, that godly character is foundational to a happy, healthy, effective life in this earth.

The simple fact is: if I make choices and act in a way that I, myself, respect ... I'll be pretty content with who I am. And if my choices and actions are based on godly character, then contentment is pretty well guaranteed. Since this emotion doesn't usually announce itself over a loudspeaker, I may not initially know what to call it, but I can *feel* it. Instead of my soul being in conflict with itself and with my Creator, there is unity. And in that unity with God, tranquility, wisdom, and joy literally *come to life*. Unity with God is their place of origin.

So, the day that I recognized an element of this inner contentment was a bit of a "red letter event." Especially after the interminable decades of going through the "rubber band effect" with God—constantly alternating between closeness and distance. Up until then, my soul had been tossed around on the stormy seas of addiction, unrest, mental agitation, physical disease, and spiritual division.

What I've noticed is that doing what is right (godly character) has a tendency to snowball into the greater good. By the same token, doing what is wrong snowballs into habitual negativity and ultimate destruction. Step Eight is about doing what is right. Taking responsibility for my choices may not be simple or easy, but it's the right thing to do.

God explains it beautifully through a verse in Ecclesiastes: "All has been heard; the end of the matter is: Fear God [revere and worship Him, knowing that He is] and keep His commandments, for this is the whole of man [the full, original purpose of his creation, the object of God's providence, the root of character, the foundation of all happiness, the adjustment to all inharmonious circumstances and conditions under the sun] *and* the whole [duty] for every man" (Ecclesiastes 12:13 AMPC).

To fear God is to show deep *respect* for Him. And this simple focus, accompanied by corresponding actions, has become my purpose in life. It's the starting point for my character, the source of my happiness, the doorway to accepting life on life's terms (from the *Big Book*)[28], and the fulfillment of obligation to my Creator. This is largely what the Twelve Step program is about, and carrying out Step

Eight is one giant way to demonstrate that deep respect for God, as it simultaneously adds to my character. Win-win.

Sound simple? Or does it sound complicated? Have you noticed that life can be simple and complicated at the same time? I certainly have. The best way I have found to deal with this dilemma is to take it one day at a time, doing what I know to do to the best of my ability. I let God take care of the rest.

So, that brings me to the second part of this Step, which is to *become willing* to make amends to those people on my list. It's hard enough to come up with "the list," but it's often harder to get to the place where I'm ready to follow through. What keeps me going in this kind of challenge is a determination to find recovery in every area of my life. I don't have any desire to live the rest of my days as a sick, dysfunctional, unhappy human being. I've had enough misery, thank you. And I recognize that, personally, I am highly motivated by that desire to be whole. If I have to go through some tough stuff to secure happiness and lasting peace, I'm okay with that. The tough places just make me more dependent on God, and that's a good thing.

So, willingness is exactly what it says it is: An act of the will.

In being willing to make amends, the hardest part for me has always been my own unforgiveness. As in holding a grudge against someone. That's a very real challenge because of the fact that offenses are frequently two-sided—two people hurting and offending each other. I don't like grudges. I never have. But sometimes I go there anyway. A useful part of Step Eight is taking the opportunity to ask myself *why*. Why am I withholding forgiveness? Why does it make my blood boil every time I think about what that person did? What purpose does it serve to hang on to this grudge? All good questions.

Relationships can be messy. What can I say? As a result, I can end up rationalizing my unwillingness to make amends because I don't want to experience more hurt. After all, don't I have the right to protect myself? There is a place of "justified anger" that, in all honesty, makes us feel more powerful and less vulnerable. And when fear lies underneath the anger, things can get that much more complicated. Isn't that usually the dynamic going on when we hold a grudge? Are we not trying to protect ourselves by staying angry? It's true that our anger is sometimes justified; a lot of things that happen in this world are unjust, and we can feel mistreated and abused. But the problem arises when we use fear and anger to create *distance*, hanging onto those emotions for all the wrong reasons.

That's when I'm tempted to vow, "I'm not going to give them the opportunity to hurt me or use me *ever again*."

At times, we do need to make a judgment call. There is definitely a place for using wisdom, and I don't believe God expects us to put ourselves in harm's way in some human effort to prove our fearlessness. But my personal efforts in emotional self-protection almost always create walls that shut me in and shut others out. I may feel somewhat safer, but I can also end up isolated and blocking the love that God and others are trying to give. So, instead of me trying to protect myself, I'm learning to allow God to protect me. That involves me lowering my walls *by faith* and asking Him for wisdom and for emotional safety. I'm finding out that He wants to do this, just as a good father wants to protect his children in every way. That doesn't mean I'll never get hurt, but it does mean that

God will walk me through the pain, comfort my heart, and wash away the residual effects.

Ultimately, when I recognize a strong resistance to forgiving some-one and making amends, it may be appropriate to first ask God if my heart needs to be healed. If my heart is still full of pain, those tasks can become extremely difficult. God is very aware of this pattern of thought and emotion, and He is more than capable of provid-ing the remedy. But I also believe that God wants me to *ask* for His healing and be willing to receive that healing and release the pain. And He wants me to pray for the other person involved because He knows that those prayers will change my heart toward them. At that point, it's much easier to look at my responsibility and be willing to make amends. However, it's also true that my heart doesn't have to be *completely* healed before I can become willing to seek resolution. Always waiting for that completion would make it way too easy to procrastinate. As with most things ... there is a balance.

The situation with my mom provided a really good lesson in this regard. She and I had such a tough time when I was growing up, being frequently at odds with each other. My rebellion and her frus-tration, a detachment disorder that neither of us knew about, and all the stressors of an alcoholic family system added to our challenges. I was absolutely convinced that she did not love me, and my response to that perceived rejection was a defiant attitude. I don't specifically remember this, but my sister tells me that Mom would remind me to pick up the toys in the "den," which was one of my chores in grade school. I would continue to sit on the couch watching television until she repeated herself two more times, and I got myself in "hot water." I was in hot water a lot. It was *defiance* practiced over and over again, and it's no wonder we didn't get along. Unfortunately, in the absence of intervention, our relationship difficulties escalated over the years, and by the time I was in high school, it was close to being "all-out war."

After I got married and had children, the situation may have softened a bit. But by the age of thirty-seven when I started counseling with Ann, the interactions with Mom were still strained and often tense. My heart was full of pain, and I was having a lot of difficulty forgiving the actual, and perceived, offenses. I had given *very little thought* to anything I may have done to harm *her*, so being willing to make amends wasn't even a consideration.

... Until Ann helped me develop another perspective.

Change the angle of your view, and the person or situation can look completely different. A head-on view of a horse has very little similarity to a side-view. You can see so much more of the total figure of the horse from the side, as compared to the front. So, because I had been in "head-to-head combat" with Mom for a long time, Ann would ask me gentle questions that caused me to observe alternate sides of the situation. Like, "Why do you think your mom made that choice?" Or, "What do you think your mom was feeling in that circumstance?" Ann helped me reframe my mental and emotional view of Mom, largely by *humanizing* her. Kids sometimes have a tendency to misinterpret motivations and have tunnel vision in regard to who their parents are as people—until they face the realization that parents struggle, hurt, and make mistakes just as they do.

Please don't be deceived: time does not heal the heart. God does.

And God has all the tools to get the job done when we cooperate.

God used my counselor to help me break through a wall of hurt and stubborn resistance. My heart had become hardened toward my mother, and God had to soften it, so I could heal and forgive. As that happened, I was then able to look at my own offenses and approach the topic of making amends.

I was in my fifties before that happened. Mom and I had, thankfully, come to a place where we were able to have some carefully navigated conversations concerning the past. We were both a bit leery, but sometimes you jump in regardless. She actually initiated some amends toward me, which then opened a very natural door for me to reach out in kind. So, over a cup of coffee, I shared remembrances of my resistant behavior and offered scenarios of the frustrations that must have created for her. As a young girl, I was either sweet and helpful … or a brat. Mom saw the latter side more frequently. We were even able to smile and laugh over some of the shenanigans I pulled, while maintaining some semblance of focus on the importance of the issues we were discussing.

I also brought up the abortion. I related the "new" viewpoints acquired over the years as I had looked at the multi-faceted situation, along with everything going on with our family during that time. It was not all pleasant to remember or talk about, but that is sometimes part of cleansing the wound. Most importantly, I took responsibility for my choices and let her know that I had purposed to "walk in her shoes." I had realized that the summer I got pregnant, with all the combined circumstances, had been an insane pressure cooker for her. I asked her forgiveness for my part in it. I'd have to say that the conversation went well, and since then, Mom and I have had similar discussions as the need arose or the opportunity availed itself, each one being of benefit to us both.

I've decided that recovery is the great adventure. There's something new and challenging around every corner. And if I were powerless and alone, that may be perceived as scary and unwelcome; but thankfully, I'm not alone. Even Frodo, on his epic journey in *The Lord of the Rings*, had Samwise Gamgee by his side. On *my* epic journey, I have my Higher Power, Jesus, and genuine support from a host of other people who identify with my struggles and my weaknesses. As I recover in community, I can embrace the love that is offered, then turn around and give it to someone else. Meanwhile, God has promised to never leave me and to be constantly at my side, willing to assist in every endeavor—if I only reach out and ask Him. He helped me make my first list of names, and He helped me remove the barriers to becoming willing to make amends. I don't have to do any of this on my own, or in my own strength.

If that were the case ... there would be no real hope of healing or of lasting peace.

Step Nine:
It's Called Personal
Responsibility

IT WAS A DEFINING MOMENT.

We've all had them at various times and for various reasons, but for me, this one was huge. As I sat in that first AA meeting back in 2013, the curtain in my heart opened up to a revelation that couldn't be denied: there was only one way to be free from my tormented existence. I had to be willing to live the way God directed me to live. And I had to fully agree with God's right to be in total authority over my life. He's boss, and I'm not. I suddenly knew this component was absolutely essential to my recovery, and without it, my healing journey would go nowhere.

Thus, after forty years of addiction, I finally got into agreement with God. I had experienced more than enough pain, and I allowed my soul to be stripped down to nothing but obedience. And I was happy. I don't think I've ever been as humble or happy as I was in that moment. If emotions can move through your bloodstream, relief and joy coursed through my veins that day. And I have never been the same. I also had a feeling this new resolution would be put to the test.

It was.

If I wasn't committed to obeying God, Step Nine is one of those Steps that I could gloss over and rationalize my way out of quite easily. And even then, it's still tempting to put it off and procrastinate. But as I'm learning to surrender everything to Jesus, it really helps to remember that He exhibited the highest level of humility that I will ever see on this earth. Being God, Himself, He came to earth to live among us and then chose to die for us. And, to me, that means His Lordship is never based on tyranny or oppression, but on love. He always wants the best for me, no matter what the circumstance, and I can put my complete trust in Him. Therefore, when He asks me to do something that feels difficult, like Step Nine, I can fully believe that He will help me, and the end result will be far better than I ever imagined.

Let's review some highlights as we work our way up to this next leg of the journey. We started with our own powerlessness and the acknowledgment of our need for help. Then we made the choice to put our hope in *God's* power and in His willingness to restore us to sane living, followed by the decision to daily surrender our wills and our lives to this loving God. Next, we begin to examine our thoughts, emotions, actions, choices, habits, patterns, and motivations and then bravely share those discoveries with God, ourselves, and one other person.

Upon seeing the futility of hanging on to these old ways, we begin to prepare ourselves to let them go, then we humbly ask God to remove these character defects—these negative ways of thinking, speaking, acting, and living. Turning to our relationships, we then make a list of all the people we have hurt during our "season of insanity," however long that may have been, in preparation for Step Nine which says: *Made direct amends to such people wherever possible, except when to do so would injure them or others.*[29]

I don't think anyone would argue that, most of the time, apologizing to someone is not an easy thing to do. Taking ownership of our mistakes may not be a piece of cake, either. And doing both things together often requires supernatural assistance from God.

Welcome to Step Nine.

The first thing I want to say about Step Nine is that there are eight other Steps in front of it, and there is a very good reason for that. Step Nine can be pretty overwhelming without the elements of willingness, courage, and faith. Steps One through Eight help us practice those elements and get a little experience under our belts, as well as a little emotional maturity. My view is that the Steps build one upon the next to progressively bring us to greater levels of healing, wholeness, and freedom. It's really hard to jump into Step Nine without the groundwork that is laid in the preceding strides of recovery.

Most or all of us have seen news stories on TV about train wrecks where multiple railroad cars have been violently thrown off the tracks. The crash site is filled with chaos and tons of debris, as smoke and dust fill the air. When the first responders arrive, they have to evaluate the situation, locate the survivors, and diffuse any remaining fire or explosive hazards. Once the people have been rescued and evacuated, the next step is cleanup. And it's always a big job.

Okay, so maybe you know where I'm going with this. How many of us feel, at least on some level, that our lives have or had turned into a train wreck? That certainly describes my state of mind and emotion when I turned to the Twelve Step program. The wreckage was everywhere, and working the Steps became my rescue and cleanup process. But before my "railroad cars" could be put back on the track where they rightfully belonged, I had to sort through the mess. Step Nine is where I focused on "cleaning up" my relationships, as I chose to deal with what had happened, along with the repercussions of my choices.

Taking responsibility for our mistakes is a big deal to God and is also designed to counteract one of the biggest character defects of addiction ... *blame shifting*. I lost count a long time ago of how many times I excused my own behavior by blaming someone else. When I was blaming, I didn't even see what my part had been. It was like wearing blinders that kept me focused on others instead of looking into a mirror at myself. My parents and my first husband got a big chunk of that finger pointing. And after a certain amount of repetition, blame shifting became a habit. I would do it mindlessly and effortlessly. I was in autopilot and didn't even know it. But God knew it, and He has kindly and gently addressed this issue in my life over a period of years. The temptation still comes at times to blame others when I have done something wrong, and I am by no means perfect in this, but I am learning to choose the higher road. I'm learning to be responsible.

And taking responsibility is the spirit of Step Nine.

Over the years, I have made amends to many people, including my mom, my boyfriends from high school and college, my grandmother, other church members, coworkers, myself, and even one of my cats. But some of my hardest amends were with the people I love the most because they were the ones who suffered the most from my addictions. Both of my kids got to watch me isolate, binge on junk food repeatedly, and contribute to the demise of my marriage and our family. With them, I was overly strict at times, controlling at times, manipulative at times, neglectful at times, an absentee mom at times, distant at times, legalistic, perfectionistic, and a supremely bad cook. What can I say? There were a couple of years when, if I hadn't taught my daughter how to fix hot dogs and mac and cheese, my kids would have been frequently eating a bowl of Fruit Loops for supper. There was a lot of "stuff" to clean up with them. I especially needed to address moving back and forth between Maryland and Kansas three times in four years. And they were in school during those years. It was a mess, and so was I.

With my first husband, I was so completely codependent that it's a wonder we ever got along. We both had active addictions and a ton of fear in our lives. But I'd have to say my biggest offense toward him was that I never learned how to trust God and His Word, instead of giving in to my emotions. I can't even begin to tell you how much trouble I got myself into because of that character defect. Since our divorce, my hindsight has much improved, and I have truly wanted to come to a place of resolution with this man who was such a big part of my life for twenty-five years. My hope was to speak with him in person, but his refusal to talk has made a one-on-one virtually impossible.

... Which conveniently brings me to the next segment on *how* to make amends.

The main options are pretty obvious. Usually, but not always, the first and best option is that you sit down with the person face-to-face. If that's not possible, then you can talk on the phone, have a Zoom meeting on your computer, or have FaceTime on an iPhone. If that's not possible, then you can write a letter or an email, but only if you're really good at conveying your thoughts and emotions with the written word. A lot can be misconstrued, otherwise. I would not recommend texting in any form, and a Western Union telegram probably wouldn't cut it either. The last resort for amends would be sending smoke signals from a distant mountaintop; if that's the only option you have, it's better than nothing. The goal is intentional communication with self-responsibility and apology—without excuses, blame shifting, or pointing out what the other person did wrong.

Amends, of course, need to be made with kindness, thoughtfulness, wisdom, good judgment, God's words, and in God's timing. And it's beneficial, but not absolutely necessary, to make amends after you have made the choice to forgive the other person for any harm they caused you. Unresolved hurt and resentment will not create the appropriate attitude or atmosphere for making sincere apologies. So, it's better to purposefully seek and receive God's healing for your heart. Once you are ready, and have committed to making your amends, you'll find that God may even set up a divine appointment with a certain someone, so the whole thing happens easily and naturally. Please don't underestimate God in any of this. He can do amazing things.

Then there is something called "living amends." I had to do this with my daughter. The short version of the story is that, in a particularly sensitive situation, I was being controlling and critical toward her, and I ended up crushing her emotionally. This was after an already long history of difficulties in our relationship. She was so wounded that she would barely talk to me and did so only if she had to. I knew beyond the shadow of a doubt that I was in deep, deep trouble. If I didn't completely change my approach with her, I was going to lose my daughter. I did apologize to her with words, but her face was like stone, and she hardly looked at me. What followed however, over the course of about two years, was a miracle. God transformed me from the inside out.

I have purposed to not say a critical word to my daughter since the fall of 2006. I have had to be truthful at times, with kindness, but God made it abundantly clear that what she needed from me was all the acceptance and approval I was not able to give to her when she was growing up. With God's help, that's what I've been doing to the best of my ability. And I have learned that there are certain offenses that just can't be made right with words; they can only be made right with actions. And sometimes they require repeated, consistent, God-directed actions over a long period of time. I have never regretted one positive word that I have said to my daughter. I'm just glad for the fact that I have a daughter who wants to be in my life. Because of God, she and I have a better relationship than we ever had in the past. She loves me, confides in me, and now considers me a safe person to come to with her most difficult problems, largely because she knows that my love for her is unconditional.

On occasion, there may be a situation in which amends could be detrimental to the person you have hurt. If your offense is actually unknown to the other person, and divulging the details would end up being emotionally cruel, a better choice would be to take the offense to God and your sponsor, pastor, or trusted friend. Another scenario is when the person you offended is someone you need to stay away from for a variety of reasons. For instance, someone who may pull you back into compromise or temptation if you were around them again. The rule of thumb is: when in doubt about making amends to a particular person, ask God in prayer, and get advice from someone else who will give wise counsel and godly support.

So, what about making amends to someone who is deceased?

I have run into a lot of people who were passengers in the same boat that I boarded back in 1976. I had been a Christian for less than two years when I realized the desperate need to ask someone to forgive me. The only problem was ... the person had died three years prior. This was all coming to the surface due to some excellent teaching I was hearing at church on forgiveness. And during those lessons, I had one person who kept coming up in my heart over and over again: my Grandmother Thelma.

Early in 1973, she was diagnosed with stomach cancer. I was eighteen years old and about four months out from the abortion, so the news of her illness was one more challenging detail on a plate that was already full. And, typical of our family at that time, no one talked about it. Dad's drinking was at an all-time high; Mom was completely overwhelmed; and I was emotionally empty and physically ill. Not long after the abortion, my body started succumbing to whatever virus was floating around. There seemed to be little resistance to colds, stomach flu, respiratory viruses, as well as chronic, severe diarrhea. And, not knowing God, the downward spiral into depression and self-hatred had begun in earnest. I was not in good shape.

At the time, Mom was working at the public library, still running a household, and at her wits end with Dad, so I can just imagine the weight she was already carrying when she found out her mother was dying. I don't even remember anyone saying that Grandmother Thelma was dying, but I might have missed the conversation. Even though I saw Grandmother several times that spring, there was, unfortunately, no meaningful interaction with her. "Warm and fuzzy" are two words that would never be used to describe my grandmother, and although I had respect for her, our relationship wasn't that close.

In early May, she called Mom and asked that my sister and I come over to provide assistance with her spring cleaning. She was a meticulous housekeeper, and her deep cleaning routine was an annual event. Apparently, that year was to be no different than any other year. As for me, I hated housecleaning. I'd rather mow grass or dig a ditch than clean house. But my sister and I, of course, went over to help Grandmother Thelma. She participated as much as she could but had to lie down a time or two to deal with pain and fatigue. Even so, as a small thank you, she cooked her famous fried porkchops and provided lunch for us. What I especially remember, however, is the horrible attitude I had. I didn't smile. I didn't talk. I just did the work, ate a porkchop, and left. I was preoccupied. I was resentful. I was terrible.

Two months later she was gone.

In the fall of 1976, while sitting under the teaching on forgiveness, I was totally convicted regarding my self-centered behavior and cried out to God to forgive me. But, what about Grandmother Thelma? How do you talk to someone who has already died? I regretfully concluded that it was an impossible situation to resolve, and I would have to carry the guilt to the end of my days. But I prayed and asked God for his help anyway. I didn't know if there was an answer to this dilemma, but I had to try.

Not long after, God answered me in the night hours. I didn't ask for a dream by any means, but that's what He provided to bring resolution. In the dream, I was at the home of my best friend from grade school. There was a bedroom in the middle of their home, occupied by the eldest sister, and I was in that room sitting alone on the side of the twin bed. I have no idea why I was in that particular house or bedroom, but there I was. As I was sitting there, upset and distraught, suddenly someone walked into the room. When I looked up, I was very surprised to see my Grandmother Thelma strolling in, looking healthy and content. She was obviously there on purpose and came to sit on the bed right beside me.

Matter-of-factly, she said, "I heard you wanted to talk to me."

I choked out, "Oh, yes!" And proceeded to tell her how horrible I felt about the way I treated her in those last several months and asked if she could ever forgive me.

She seemed completely calm and comfortable, like this interchange was a regular part of her day and nothing out of the ordinary. "Absolutely peaceful" is the only way to describe her demeanor.

Looking at me kindly, and smiling just a little, she responded, "It's okay. I forgive you."

That was it. That's all she needed to say. Relief washed over me like a warm spring shower, and I thanked her with all the sincerity in my heart. Then, after stating it was time to go, she stood up and walked out of the room. With her departure, I woke up.

I have no concrete explanation for it, but from that day forward, the matter was settled. I had no more guilt, no more remorse, and total peace. I knew that all was well between my grandmother and me and that the next time I saw her, we would hug each other freely and joyfully. Something very spiritual and very real had transpired in that dream.

And God was smiling.

Now, I'm not saying this is God's standard response to all such issues; it's just how He chose to deal with me. What I do believe is that God will tailor His help to your particular need, whatever it may be, and you will find the answer that brings peace. If you ask.

At this juncture, I'd like to switch gears a bit and bring up something that hasn't yet been thoroughly discussed: the recognition of *feelings and emotions*. To some people, that may sound elementary and unnecessary, but not so for addicts and those who have lived in dysfunctional family systems. And I bring it up at this point because making amends *revolves* around those elements.

They are the nucleus of the need.

God has feelings and emotions, and He made us in His image. We obviously have them, and some of us are completely ruled by them. However, a common symptom of addiction and dysfunction is the inability to recognize and deal with emotions in a healthy way. Identifying feelings is not an innate skill, it has to be learned. And when we grow up in an environment that creates a lot of negative emotions, we actually learn to avoid them, cover them up, ignore them, and basically run away from them in any way we can. Why? Because we don't know what to do with them. It's painful. As a child, or an adult, when we get overloaded with pain and don't have the learned skills to handle them ... they handle us.

My experience was very common. The difficulties in my home and close relationships led to unresolved hurt, anger, abandonment, depression, and fear. This was true as a child and an adult, not every moment of every day, but often enough. In the midst of those challenging emotions, the discomfort felt like it would go on for an eternity. The world felt scary and out of control, and I felt completely alone in trying to deal with it. So, escape became my auto-response. At a very young age, I started using food for emotional comfort and television for mental distraction. In later years I added the romance books. Corporately, as well as individually, they took off the "edge." Over time, what started out as dysfunctional responses became negative habits, then addictions.

Dysfunctional, addicted home environments don't encourage the expression of emotion, except maybe anger. This is true for all the family members, but often especially true for the males in the household. Usually, no one really knows how to effectively discuss and resolve emotions or the issues that create them, and the unspoken rule is to ignore "them." Whatever "them" is. Just don't talk about them, and they might go away. But they very seldom do. So, we closet our emotional pain and unconsciously look for pain killers. We try to meet our needs through substances and behaviors that anesthetize. But unfortunately, our choices frequently end up hurting the people with whom we interact, as well as ourselves.

Thus, the necessity of working Steps Four through Nine.

In the middle of our damage, we damage others, then amends have to be made in order to bring resolution and peace. It's not rocket science, but no one in recovery will tell you that it's fun or easy. When I first began to learn these things in counseling and support groups, I was determined to help my kids walk down a different pathway than the one I had traveled. If you asked them, they would wryly smile and agree that we had emotion-recognition "training" at our house. When there was an upset at home, or at school, I would ask, "Okay, what are you feeling? Why do you think you're feeling that? What do you think the other person is feeling?" I coached them and taught them to look underneath the surface. The more obvious emotions on the surface are often the tip of the iceberg, so we talked about root causes. They probably got tired of it all, but I felt it was a definite first step in handling life in a healthier way. And I had resolved within myself that this dysfunction would *stop* in my generation.

Now, as adults, they tease me sometimes about my efforts, but they also express gratitude. I'm hoping it was one of the things I did right.

The same issue of emotions also needs to be examined from a spiritual standpoint. God knows we have a wide variety of human feelings, but He doesn't want them to dominate our behavior. I used to fall into the category of being pushed around by every emotional whim. Whatever emotion surfaced in my soul became my master. Its "wish" was my command, whether it be joy, sadness, depression, hurt, fear, anger, self-pity, frustration, giddiness, discouragement, irritation, anxiety, or despair. If it showed up, I yielded to it. I do not recommend that mode of living to anyone on the planet.

God brought this lesson home to me through the book of James one day. Chapter one, verses five through eight in the Amplified Classic version say, "If any of you is deficient in wisdom, let him ask of the giving God [Who gives] to everyone liberally and ungrudgingly, without reproaching or faultfinding, and it will be given him. Only it must be in faith that he asks with no wavering (no hesitating, no doubting). For the one who wavers (hesitate, doubts) is like the billowing surge out at sea that is blown hither and thither and tossed by the wind. For truly, let not such a person imagine that he will receive anything [he asks for] from the Lord, [For being as he is] a man of two minds (hesitating, dubious, irresolute), [he is] unstable and unreliable and uncertain about everything [he thinks, feels, decides]" (James 1:5–8, AMPC).

As I was reading that passage during my quiet time that day, I got to the part about being "tossed by the wind," and God intercepted my thoughts and changed the words to "tossed by the winds of emotion." It then became crystal clear that allowing my emotions to rule my life was pushing me around all over the place. I was being tossed here, there, and everywhere, while it made me unstable, unreliable, full of doubt, double-minded, lacking in faith and, in essence, a *Flake*. No wonder it was hard for me to make decisions. I was basing them on my emotions, and when my emotions changed in the next hour or on the following day, my decisions would change. I couldn't stick to anything. I also realized that true wisdom is based on the Word of God and captained by the Spirit of God. Being led by my emotions caused me to make very unwise decisions and added to my struggle with trust.

That revelation was the beginning of change. It takes time to change a lifelong habit, but with God's help, it can be done. I had to learn that God can not only heal my emotions but also show me how to deal with them in a constructive manner. Rule number one: don't let them dictate your choices. Rule number two: acknowledge them and take them to God. Rule number three: talk about them if you need to and ignore them if you don't. They will change in about fifteen minutes anyway.

And there you have my version of *Emotions 101*. No extra charge.

As I'm learning how to successfully deal with emotions, I have more stability, balance, and peace in my life. I'm also less offensive to others. I don't say as many things that are angry or hurtful or based on self-pity. I can tell when I'm trying to manipulate and control, and I purpose to go in a different direction. I have the presence of mind to think before I speak. And I don't feel pushed to act out addictively in an effort to cover up. All of that makes me easier to live with and generally easier to be around.

I still have to apply Step Nine at times, but not as often.

As we wrap up, one of the most important things to remember about making amends is that we have to leave the results in the hands of God. I am not responsible for someone else's response to my apology; I am only responsible to make the amends in the way God asks me to. If I have certain expectations of the other person when I apologize, and my expectations are not met, then I'm setting myself up for disappointment, hurt, or even relapse. How they choose to respond is between them and God alone.

And at this point, I have to reiterate that Step Nine is not about what the other person has or hasn't done to you. It's about what you did or neglected to do to them. This is not at all to overlook or minimize what someone else did, but in the Twelve Steps, there is a major emphasis on walking out humility and taking responsibility for our own actions—and less of a focus on what others have done. However, because of its importance, *forgiving others* is a life-changing topic to be discussed in a later chapter.

Another good thing to keep in mind is the fact that only God can absolve our guilt. That word, absolve, means: to set or declare (someone) free from blame, guilt, or responsibility. It means to pardon, exonerate, and/or release.[30] God took care of our sin-guilt through the death of Jesus on the cross, confirmed by 1 Peter 2:24: "He personally bore our sins in His [own] body on the tree [as on an altar and offered Himself on it], that we might die (cease to exist) to sin and live to righteousness. By His wounds you have been healed" (AMPC).

We can't look to the person we hurt or offended to absolve our guilt. It's not their job, and if we give them that power, we may create a boatload of pain. When we carry out the responsibility God puts in our hands by making amends, and let Him declare us free from guilt, Step Nine does the work it was designed to accomplish. We are able to resolve situations where we violated a standard of conduct and often our own conscience while offending and hurting others in the process. It's truly a gift to be able to lay down that burden once and for all.

As you walk through the Steps, keep in mind that this *is* a walk of faith. If we could do the Steps in our own strength, we wouldn't need God. And if we didn't need God, we would never learn the healthy dependence that is necessary to form a bedrock of trust in our lives. Hopefully, I'll never lose the sense of amazement that I have right now when I think about the huge difference this has made. Putting my trust in a Power much greater than myself *is* the essence of faith.

He has enabled me to do things I thought I would never be able to do … and that's a big reason why I call myself a *grateful*, recovering addict.

Step Ten:
Daily Maintenance

2020: THE YEAR OF INFAMY.

A worldwide pandemic, masks and social distancing, a U.S. presidential election equaled by no other, political dissention of epic proportions, a barrage of inflammatory rhetoric, racial riots, urban violence, forest fires wreaking havoc, multiple hurricanes and tropical storms, one national "earthquake" after another that rocked our world and left us reeling. I've lived through a fair number of decades, but I've never experienced a year such as this.

And it was also the year that I rocked my personal world with a relapse.

In comparison with national and world events, that could sound like a small thing. But not when addiction creates death in all its different forms. Actually, hindsight reveals that I had been having smaller relapses for quite a while, but my life was in such high gear that I didn't pause long enough to accurately assess the predicament. Before the months of relapse, as I was making my way through three years of monumental change in almost every area of life, I slowly began to allow compromises and "slips" that opened the door to a major backslide. Then, suddenly my husband and I were launched into a brand-new business, we were all thrown into the middle of a pandemic, and I was at home alone on a frequent basis over a long period of time. Strange things can happen to a recovering addict when you're at home alone.

In all fairness, a lot of people cooped up at home during the pandemic gained weight. I just didn't want to be one of them. And, even though it was only eight pounds, for me it was double-dangerous. There's a difference between temporary overeating and addiction. I was having what I called "kitchen binges" where you just go eat whatever is available, not because of hunger, but because it's a compulsive response to life. And you keep going back and going back until you're beyond full and feeling physically, spiritually, mentally, and emotionally ill. This is quickly followed by the all-too-familiar shame and self-disgust. Then you stop, spend two or three days recovering, ask for forgiveness and determine you'll never do it again ...

And then you do it again. And again. And again.

That's when it starts getting really scary.

I thought those days were gone for good.

It just goes to show that there is truth in what the *Big Book* says. We are not cured of our addiction. We are given a "daily reprieve contingent on the maintenance of our spiritual condition."[31] Although the tendency to be compulsive remains, the compulsion lies dormant within certain parameters. God's power relieves my addictive tendencies one day at a time as I position myself in His will and practice the Steps. It's called working the Program. But if the days come and go, and I'm not doing my part, the result is that my spiritual condition deteriorates, and the power to stay clean, sober, and abstinent begins to falter. The compulsion may sit quietly for a while, but eventually, the relapse will come.

As did mine.

The bad news is that, for several months, I made myself miserable—spirit, soul, and body. The good news is that I stopped, with God's help. And I don't take "stopping" for granted. I've known or heard about too many people who relapsed, and that was the last we heard of them. They "went back out" and suffered the consequences. Some of them died. So, I thank God that sanity returned, and I had the opportunity to learn some valuable lessons. The first one being: there is a reason for Step Ten!

Before I share the lessons learned, let's take a look at this Step. It says: ***Continued to take personal inventory, and when we were wrong, promptly admitted it.***[32] Under all the right circumstances, this Tenth Step is meant to be a tool, inspired by the Biblical principle of examination, to regularly see where I am with God, with myself, and with others. This is not something I do once and call it good. This is a daily practice that helps me maintain a clean heart, which is the best way to stay balanced, keep on track, and hopefully correct myself when I veer off course. The first nine Steps of the Twelve Step program are all about discovering God, surrendering to His way of life, dealing with the past, identifying and working on character defects, and resolving relationship pain. Step Ten is like doing Steps Four through Nine in mini-form on a daily basis, and most people in successful recovery have learned to set aside a few minutes each day to accomplish this task.

... But I wasn't doing it.

I was "cruising." You know what I mean? I was sliding by, doing the bare minimum, resting on past victories, getting overly confident.

But Step Ten is all about not taking anything for granted and making regular assessments of the spiritual condition that I'm supposed to be maintaining. For the sake of clarification, my simple definition of "spiritual condition" is: a place where my heart, mind, will, thoughts, emotions, attitudes, and actions are submitted to God. None of us operate in that submission perfectly, but the idea is to stay vigilant. In my years of sobriety, I have learned to recognize the internal agitation that comes when one or more of those areas are offtrack, but I had become overly busy, sloppy, and somewhat tone-deaf.

Dangerous ground.

This is a good place to remind myself that addiction is a lifestyle. And it's my lifestyle that has to make a "one-eighty change" with the assistance of other recovering addicts and my Higher Power. So, a good question is: am I maintaining my new lifestyle?

This is where a personal, daily inventory becomes invaluable.

In past years, while living in the hotbed of addiction, there was no such thing in my life as personal inventory. The whole purpose of using food the way I did was to avoid reality and to escape pain, so examining my life and my choices wasn't even on the radar. The problem was: all of that escaping was extremely temporary, and when I finished the bag of chips, the box of frozen fruit bars, the three candy bars, and the supersized burger and fries, reality came slamming back into my mind and my emotions full force. Along with self-hatred. And with my codependency, I had only a small cache of information regarding healthy relationships and was too busy controlling, blaming, or feeling sorry for myself. As for "promptly admitting when I was wrong" ... that was a moot point. I was so consumed with shame that admitting I was wrong usually threatened to rock my universe. I had to be "right" in order to function and survive. Am I exaggerating? I only wish I were. So, maybe you can imagine the "night and day" difference that recovery, abstinence, and sanity made in my life.

They are gifts to be treasured. And ones to be protected by using the given tools.

But, even with that knowledge tucked under my belt, I missed it. What I missed is something very important called diligence. I have to be consistent and stay on guard. Not only is addiction a nemesis, but we also have an enemy whose primary goal is to destroy our lives. God provides the tools to protect us from demise, but we have to use them.

So, here's a little hindsight:

The week that I had three "kitchen binges," I started asking myself some serious questions, and the lightbulb finally came on. I realized that, once again, I was dealing with fear and a lack of trust related to several situations going on at the time. But instead of turning every-thing over to God, I had started trying to figure things out on my own. Frankly, if I had been doing a daily Step Ten, He could have revealed that to me earlier. As for fear, it can slither through areas of my life like an insidious snake, stealing my peace and creating weakness. The enemy strikes where he knows my strength can be compromised. And the truth is, for the rest of my life I will have to be extra vigilant in this area. But God wants to protect me by being my refuge, my fortress, and my place of safety. He wants me to see stumbling blocks before I fall over them and end up hurting myself and others.

Let me say again: there is a reason for Step Ten.

This Step can help me to *stop* and check out what's going on in my thoughts and feelings. This is an invaluable tool because we often have crazy schedules and are constantly pushing ourselves to the limit, at least in this country. Common sense tells me that a daily perusal of what's happening "inside" makes just as much sense as brushing my teeth on a regular basis. It's needful. When I'm at peace and have balance, the temptations generally don't come. Not nearly as often.

One lesson I learned during this relapse is how easy it is to fall back into denial and gloss over "red flags." Just ignore it, and it will go away. Addiction isn't just using a substance or behavior in a destructive way; it's a maze of mental and emotional patterns that we use to try to cope with life. I was too busy to slow down and examine the "red flags" long enough to wake up and put a halt to the insanity. So, I fell back into coping with life in ways that don't work. And clearly, I wasn't submitting my will to God on a daily basis.

Overall, what I learned through the pain of relapse is that Step Ten is largely about accountability, self-care, and appropriate responses to life. It's also about humility. In the Twelve Step program, you never become a master. About the time you think you've become a guru, life sneaks up on you, and you trip over your own two feet. What works is to maintain a sense of healthy dependence and stay submitted to the One who has all power. I need God, and I need others to successfully live each day. And I need humility to remember that I am always subject to making mistakes. Mistakes for which I might need to apologize and make amends.

... And, at one point, I had to apologize to my husband. History reveals to me that, if I binge, it leads to isolating and acting like a goofball. I get negative and self-centered and often feel sorry for myself. None of that is good for a marriage or any other personal relationship. During my relapse, my husband and I had an upset one weekend that carried into Monday, with some unwise and unkind things being said. We were both suffering. After getting desperate enough to go to a Twelve Step group that I don't usually attend, it suddenly dawned on me that I had had a binge on the Friday before the weekend. It all became crystal clear how things went sour. I hadn't told anyone, including my husband, about the binge. I had kept it a secret.

When the "season of bingeing" first started, I was confessing to my husband after each incident. I would talk out my anxiety and frustration with him and basically do a Step Five. But when it turned into one repeat after another, I felt too ashamed to share. Toward the end, I realized that part of the problem was a complete lack of accountability. Who's going to see me binge? I know God can see me, but no one else will know, and I can get away with it, right?

Wrong.

It's not about who does or doesn't see me. It's about doing things God's way, not my way. Acting out compulsively and stepping back into bondage leads to death. And if I step back into the addiction, there's absolutely no guarantee that I'll come out of it. Meanwhile,

I'm separating myself from God, from other people, from my family, and from my own soul.

So, when sanity returned, I decided to make myself directly accountable to an accountability partner. My job is to text this person every evening with an honest report about my eating during that day. Their job is to simply make me accountable by receiving the text and responding appropriately. I wasn't sure this new protocol would make a big difference, but it has turned out to be very helpful. It breaks down the isolation and provides a kindly "pair of eyes" looking over my shoulder. The daily report may not be necessary forever, but for now, it has been a valuable aid in returning to a diligent practice of the Steps.

The other big lesson I learned seems embarrassingly simple. But oh-so important.

... God's care is often connected to self-care. The first component is remembering that I am turning my will and my life over to the care of God. And He has been teaching me a two-fold lesson in that regard. One is that God is my Father, and He wants to take care of me in every area of life. This is a parental care, a loving care, and an all-sufficient care. More than enough. Always available. Always trustworthy. He's not distant and vague. He's personal, up close, warm, reliable, ever present, powerful, practical, diligent, and wise. He's a living being. He is God. And I can feel absolutely safe in turning my personal power (my will) over to Him and the totality of my life to His supervision, provision, and protection.

I just have to be willing to try, one day at a time.

This understanding of God has become very important to me. It helps me trust. And I'm finding, over and over again, that most problems in my life are fear based and thus alleviated by choosing to trust. Analysis has repeatedly brought me to that conclusion.

The second component revolves around self-care. The basic idea here is to pay attention to what I'm trying to tell myself. That sounds a bit strange, but it makes sense. I need to watch for signs and signals that my body, mind, and emotions are giving me and ask myself what I need. I'm not quite sure how I missed this primary, self-care education when I was growing up, but I'm finding out that I'm not alone. This phenomenon is common among folks with addictions, and that's probably why this issue is dealt with in recovery. Sometimes, for various reasons, we learn to ignore our personal needs; we just push through and hope the need goes away. But it rarely does.

With me, one thing I started noticing was that I frequently glossed over the signals my body sent me when it was tired. I honestly don't know how or why I ever got into this habit, but I almost always forced myself to keep going. Inevitably, when I tried to barrel through the fatigue, I would just get more and more tired. That ultimately led to mental fatigue, emotional fatigue, usually some kind of self-pity, and a binge. Binges were my source of comfort. The catch is: a binge, even though temporary, does bring a certain level of comfort. Make no mistake. So, when I was feeling discomfort in any way, shape, or form, a binge was my standard response. That's why I have had to learn a *different* response.

In the end, the fix for this particular self-care issue was pretty easy. When I get tired, I rest. Sometimes, for various reasons, I can't stop to take a break, so I ask God to give me strength and endurance until the opportunity comes to do so. He sees me through. That sounds so simple that I feel kind of silly sharing this. And it tripped me up for a very long time. But it is what it is. I'm just thankful that God revealed this stumbling block, so I could make the change.

Another simple thing I have learned is that when I get a craving for something cold and sweet, I often discover that I'm actually thirsty. A nice, tall glass of cold water takes care of it. How cool is that? (No pun intended.)

And a more obvious scenario is in the emotional realm. When I first started taking concrete steps to get this book published, fear showed up almost instantly. I would get off the phone with my consultant and want to rush to the kitchen to find something to eat. And not because I was hungry. The good thing is, I knew right away what was going on and got through it with some gentle self-talk and a reminder of God's direction, power, and strength. He makes me more than adequate, and with His help, I can complete this assignment. On a few occasions, I also called my daughter to discuss my anxiety. She has become a great source of support—my own personal cheerleader—and I know beyond any doubt that God has appointed her to help me fulfill this particular purpose.

So, essentially, part of God's care, is giving me wisdom about the things I can do to take care of myself. I need to be aware, pay attention, check the grid, ask myself what's going on, and pray. God can show me all kinds of things that I can miss on my own. He knows me better than I know myself, so His intimate knowledge of me becomes a vital tool in my recovery process. The same is true of a sponsor or trusted friend. We can often lean on the people who know us well and ask them to offer their perspective concerning our self-discovery. Ultimately, the better I know myself, the better I can take care of myself in appropriate ways. Ask for help. Listen to God.

Recovery happens in community.

As we wind things down, let me just say that ... "stuff happens." And, in my decades of living, I have not found a better way to deal with everyday stuff than the consistent application of Twelve Step principles. If I don't deal with what happened yesterday, then I get to carry it into Today. And if I continue to neglect the process of dealing with what has happened day after day, then it snowballs into a big mess. That's how I lived a large portion of my previous life, and it led to active, multiple addictions and a continuing state of dysfunction. I am extremely grateful for what I am learning in the Twelve Step program because it has made a difference that is almost beyond description.

So, as "stuff happens" and I am reminded that there is very little in life that I actually control, I also remember that one thing I can control is my response. Each day I'm presented with opportunities to respond to people, situations, and circumstances; and keeping tabs on how I do that becomes a learning tool. Are my responses working? Are situations resolved effectively? Am I staying in balance and experiencing peace more often than turmoil? All good questions. And Step Ten helps me answer them.

Sometimes the "stuff" is all about relationship issues. I may open my mouth and say something when wisdom would have dictated keeping my mouth closed. Sometimes my attitude just stinks, and it affects how I respond in situations. Sometimes, through self-centeredness or oversight, I miss an opportunity to be kind, thoughtful, or compassionate. In certain cases, I get to go back to the person or persons involved and make it right. That's a part of "promptly admitting when I'm wrong."

Other times, the "stuff" points to spiritual posturing. Maybe I'm not paying enough attention to the principles of trust, humility, and dependence on God, which are three areas where I need to stay on alert. I have also learned that denial (or self-delusion) has a tendency to resurface in my areas of greatest weakness. For instance, in the area of trusting God, I can actually fool myself into thinking that I am trusting when I'm not. And then it suddenly dawns on me what I'm doing. I have to purpose to remember that I'm still growing in trust, growing in humility, and growing in a healthy dependence on God, so I often focus on readings that reinforce the importance of those elements. They are completely foundational. And even though in this life I will never totally "arrive," I'm striving to make these principles really solid in my mind and heart. God is helping me do that because I can't do it on my own. I ask for help. And I do a lot of asking.

Another area where "stuff constantly happens" is in my thoughts and emotions. I may not be able to control what thoughts come into my head, but I can control what stays there. That's a nugget of truth that's been around for centuries. In recovery groups, there is a common phrase called, "stinkin' thinkin'," and it simply describes a state of mind that takes you down the wrong path. Some folks in the Program call that frame of mind "getting up in your head." But the point is, people with addictive tendencies and addictive backgrounds (like mine) seem to have a considerable amount of trouble with their thoughts. This is a big one. In the past, I defaulted to negative thinking almost all of the time and then filled in the gaps with outright fear, dread, or self-deprecation. I blamed; I pouted; I obsessed; I worried; I fretted; I steamed; I ranted; I whined; and I browbeat myself. All very quietly in my head. And sometimes not so quietly.

It became absolutely necessary to learn a different way.

One of my biggest motivations to change in this particular area comes from knowing that my thoughts directly affect my emotions. And for me, negative emotions (especially fear) lead to negative choices. That's a huge reason to be aware of what I'm thinking, and line up my thoughts with God's Word and with the wisdom of recovery principles. Joyce Meyer says to "think about what you're thinking about" because a lot of us just let all kinds of thoughts float around in our heads and don't even realize that they are there.[33] That was definitely my old pattern.

At this point, I try to pay more attention to my thoughts and realign them with God's Truth when they become wayward. That takes a lot of practice and a lot of diligence, so I have engaged the assistance of the Holy Spirit in this endeavor! It's too big for me, alone. You would be amazed at what God is willing and able to do if you just ask. The bottom line is: when my emotions start getting out of whack, all I have to do is stop and ask myself what I'm thinking about, either consciously or subconsciously. If I can't identify it, I ask the Lord, and He usually tells me. Then I know what to address and, specifically, how to pray. If I do get stuck, which I do, I talk to someone who can be a sounding board and help me sort through it all.

And lastly, there's all sorts of other "stuff" like financial problems, political unrest, cultural upheavals, family divisions, holiday conflicts, disunity on the job, car repairs, sick kids, etc., etc.—all of which can be a genuine challenge. If I don't learn how to respond appropriately to the expected and unexpected events in life, I will be constantly off-balance and subject to the woes of instability, anxiety, and stress. Thankfully, the Twelve Step program is designed to teach me just that. With each meeting, each encounter with God, reading materials, and conversations with others in recovery, I am presented with learning experiences that show me how to respond in godly, effective ways. All I have to do is apply that knowledge and incorporate it into a new way of living.

That's all.

But no matter what's going on in me or around me, there is always an opportunity to apply the principle of gratitude. If I can be truly grateful for whatever happens, the control is placed in the hands of God, regardless of what it is, and He can make it productive and fruitful. Which brings me to the last point I want to make: Step Ten should include the acknowledgment of good. As God and others help me to assess my daily living, I can make note of the things that I actually did right. Positive reinforcement is valuable, and this Step helps me practice self-affirmation. For example, I can acknowledge the other day when I remained patient with my husband instead of losing my temper. Or I can be grateful that I stepped back to pray instead of going into a panic when I found a two-hundred-dollar discrepancy in our bank balance. And I can remember that I stopped to help an elderly woman in the grocery store retrieve an item from a shelf too high for her to reach. Big or small, taking note of what is good perpetuates more of the same.

So, as I use Step Ten to do a spiritual heart-check, examine my thoughts and feelings, take appropriate responsibility, ask for forgiveness, check my boundaries, assess my responses, and affirm the good, I have a much better chance at walking in peace and a place of learned contentment. And that's a sweet, sweet thing.

I don't know about you, but to me, that makes each day worth living.

What I love so much about this whole Program is the fact that, if you stay with it, you just keep learning and growing. There are never-ending layers of knowledge where golden nuggets of enlightenment open the door to transformation. I can confidently make that statement because I'm familiar with the nature of God and His Word. The Twelve Steps are based on God's Word and God's principles. Therefore, they have that eternal, infinite quality that characterizes the truth of God. About the time you think you've learned it all, you find out you're just getting started. There's always something else to discover. Until the day I go to be with Jesus, I will have a steady stream of opportunities to enrich my life and my soul. And I personally believe our learning continues beyond that point. But for now, I clearly understand why "old-timers" convincingly express their gratitude for this disease. Just think about it. Where else are you going to be "forced" to live a supernatural existence, to constantly grow, and to watch God do miracles in your life on a daily basis ... and then find out that you absolutely love it?

... This is discipleship at its best.

Step Eleven:
A Solid Rock Foundation

I BELIEVE GOD IS THE ANSWER.

As Christians, most or all of us believe that. But if you're like me, I was having a hard time genuinely connecting with God, and therefore connecting with the answer. So, as a Christian, I spent thirty-eight and a half years struggling through life *without* a lot of answers. It turned out that what I thought I knew of God needed some serious editing, and God Himself became my editor as I began working the Steps. Once I turned my will and my life over to Him, He started showing me who He really was. It was pretty amazing how quickly He began revealing Himself and how quickly I started seeing Truth when I got my self-will out of the way. God won't remove your self-will for you. We have to get to the place where we're willing to let it go. The motivation for "letting go" often comes through pain. The ironic advantage is: no one in Twelve Step recovery is a stranger to pain. So, I pray that your pain will lead you to humility because humility is the willingness to abide under the love and the authority of God.

In years past, I was trying to be my own god, and for a long time, I didn't even know it. I wanted to do things my way and keep things under my control mostly because I was afraid of letting anyone *else* do the job. The problem was that I was uniquely inadequate at being my own god, as we all are. It took large and prolonged doses of pain to wake me up long enough to smell the coffee. Fortunately, I love the smell of coffee. And I love what happens when I turn my will and my life over to God, and "Let God be God."

Now, I said all that to say this: Step Eleven is about a *relationship* with God. It's about something called symbiosis, where two entities interrelate in a way that is beneficial to both. This Step says: ***Sought through prayer and meditation to improve our conscious contact with God, praying only for knowledge of His will for us and the power to carry that out.***[34]

Some Christians look at this Step and say to themselves, "Oh, good. This is an easy one. I already know God and have a relationship with Him."

But as I said, being a Christian in "name" and actually being in a living relationship can be two different things. My personal goal is to seek, find, and maintain that living relationship. God really is the answer. I need Him. And without His power, I don't find wholeness. If I fall away from my power connection—God—I fall away from sobriety, peace, and balance. It's as simple as that.

So, as I began my quest to "seek, find, and maintain," I had to learn that a relationship with God is a relationship with Love. And it's a love unlike any we have ever known or experienced. That knowledge was in my head, but the enlightenment of my heart was another story. So, during a powerful season of inner healing between 2006 and 2010, God revealed several core issues that needed to be addressed. I knew from the start that they were cornerstones of truth that had never been properly formed. In fact, they had been laid incorrectly, like a slab of cracked cement, and had thus caused multiple problems. And this particular issue, which God unveiled to me one day, was a real turning point. [As a precursor, let me just say that I'm completely grateful to the Lord for knowing me well enough to use "visual aids." I am a visual learner, and He often uses real photos, word pictures, inner "visions," scenes in nature, and any other tool that will help me understand what He wants to portray.]

This particular visual aid showed up as a "picture of my heart" that formed in response to a pertinent question I had asked. It was immediately noticeable that one half of my heart looked healthy and robust, and the other half, to my dismay, was wrapped in barbed wire and chains. Quite a contrast. I was confused, to say the least, and asked the Lord what was going on. His answer orbited around something that I hadn't even thought about up until that day. He told me I needed to ask Him to come into my heart "just to let Him love me." That's how He said it. I had invited Him to come into my heart in 1975 when I was initially saved, but frankly, I was just following directions from the person who led me to the Lord. The directive was a bit vague and generic. And, at the time, I was almost totally focused on committing myself to God, with little or no thought of how He wanted to love me in return.

God, however, knew that I was already locked into believing that His love was conditional. And for many years, I subsequently tried to earn that love. But now He wanted me to fully recognize and yield to the grace and beauty of His unconditional love. Something pure, simple, and all-encompassing. And He was right. I hadn't done that at all.

Thus ... the chains and barbed wire.

What I saw next, in my mind's eye, was what appeared to be the inside of a small English cottage. It had a low ceiling; a fireplace with a warm, crackling fire; a small round table and two chairs; curtains framing a glass-paned window; and a heavy wooden door—thick and well built. I was standing in the middle of the room when I heard a knock on the door, and I knew immediately who was on the other side. I walked to the door, opened it ...

And found myself looking into the eyes of Jesus.

There was something about Him that was completely open, completely accepting, and completely approachable. In a split second, the thought danced across my mind that this was the same Jesus who walked on the earth in human form, preaching, ministering, and reaching out to touch hearts and draw them into the Kingdom. People flocked to Him in those special days of His earthly ministry. And whether they could put it into words or not, there was something magnetic about this Man. Yes, He healed them. Yes, He taught them. But there was more ... Jesus was love personified. They just wanted to be in His presence.

That's the Jesus who stood in my doorway.

And that's the love I saw in His eyes.

It enveloped me like a cloak. I knew this love was everything I had ever wanted or needed. That God, through Jesus, had found a way to make me His. To hold me close forever. I could feel God seeking me out, calling to me, coming to where I was, and not demanding that I somehow find my way to Him. This was a love that I had always dreamed about and longed for. A love that never ends, never fluctuates, never betrays, never changes, never gives up, never stops caring, and is never diminished. I knew in that moment that His love for me was absolutely unconditional and always had been. It wasn't based on anything I did or didn't do, or on any other condition. There were no conditions. There was no pressure to perform, no fear of losing it, and no fear of not being worthy. I knew His love was mine forever. Never to be lost. Always to be found.

This was God. This was Jesus. This was love.

As I looked into His eyes, I knew that the next step was mine. I could let Him remain on the other side of the threshold, or I could invite Him in. And I knew that this encounter was all about asking Him into my heart "just to love me." To actively and intentionally receive His love in the fullness of the revelation that had just been given.

With no hesitation, I extended the invitation.

And His face broke into this beautiful smile that seemed to reach into my heart, gently opening every corner and crevice to an indescribable warmth. He walked into the room and stood there looking at me with His arms wide open and beckoning. He was waiting for me to step within the circle. And I almost ran. As His arms gently surrounded me, the power and strength that began flowing through me brought a steady stream of tears. I could physically feel it pouring in, unrestrained and unfettered.

For the first time, I felt no need to earn what was so freely given. I understood. Like a newborn babe with absolutely nothing to give in return, I simply received. I turned off the whispering lies of inadequacy. Of being unlovable and undeserving. My Father was loving me just because He created me. Just because He wanted to. Just because that's who He is. And, oh, what a love He has. It always reaches out, always shows up, always provides, always fills to the full. It believes the best and walks in incredible patience. It sees through the eyes of faith, as it listens, supports, creates good, and gives good. His love is continuously extended to me; never withheld. I am covered, protected, and surrounded by a shield. I am hidden in times of danger, always secure and always safe. Things can happen around me and outside of me, but on the inside, I am standing on the solid rock foundation of His love, sure and eternal.

Ephesians 3:16–19 says it beautifully:

"I pray that from his glorious, unlimited resources he will empower you with inner strength through his Spirit. Then Christ will make his home in your hearts as you trust in him. Your roots will grow down into God's love and keep you strong. And may you have the power to understand, as all God's people should, how wide, how long, how high, and how deep his love is. May you experience the love of Christ, though it is too great to understand fully. Then you will be made complete with all the fullness of life and power that comes from God" (Ephesians 3:16–9, NLT).

That says it all.

God's Love, and Strength, and Power go together in one package.

I have learned that this is what enables me to completely open my heart to Him. And the more I let Him into my heart and my life, the more He can mold me and change me into who He created me to be. I have also discovered that the more I let His love heal me and make me complete, the more I want to give that love away and help others. It all makes perfect sense. If we are becoming more and more like God, as we let Him change us, then our innate response is to love others just as He has loved us. He is blessed. We are blessed. And we do it over, and over, and over again.

This is symbiosis.

And it's great stuff.

Now, as we switch gears and approach this living relationship from a practical viewpoint, let's take a moment to discuss some of the effective tools that can be used to reach the goal. Step Eleven talks about using prayer and meditation "to improve our conscious contact with God." Prayer is a well-known component in our interaction with God, and I have often heard other people talk about the wonderful times they've had in communion with the Lord. Their joy was obvious, and I was a little envious. Because, in all honesty, I can well remember the days and years when praying was methodical, tedious, and mostly dry, except on the rare occasion. As you can imagine, I was not highly motivated to pursue that pastime. I'm embarrassed by that confession, but I share it with the instinctive knowledge that I'm not alone in such struggles. Back then, I didn't properly understand the purpose of prayer. Like other aspects of my previous walk with God, I mistakenly connected prayer with "earning points" and getting some of the love that I was wanting.

But the richness is in relationship, not in religious duty.

The other problem was that I wasn't in a good place positionally. I had concluded that my chances of being close to God were already blocked by my sin and sickness. And, after many years in active addiction, my guilt and condemnation also perpetuated the need to stay at a distance. Maybe I just didn't want to know that my sin was in plain sight. Overall, I was also aware on some level that a consistent, viable relationship with the Lord required something that I didn't have at the time: humility, trust, and a strong belief in His grace. And I think I only knew that much because God was gracious enough to give me a glimpse.

Thankfully, my current approach is different because I have learned that the reward of prayer and meditation is the very treasure that I had wanted all along. Jeremiah 29 says that if we seek Him and require Him as a vital necessity, we will find Him when we search for Him with all our heart (Jeremiah 29:13, AMPC). How would you like to "find God"? I remember having that exact desire long before I got saved. In fact, God used that desire to draw me into His Kingdom. It's really no different than finding genuine love with another human being. The relationship grows through attention, time together, conversation, shared experiences, common goals, mutual caring, and mutual commitment. I love God, and I love to bless Him. He feels the same way about me. So, today, my prayers are pretty simple: I adore you, God. Please help me; please show me Your will; please give me wisdom. I commit my life to you, Jesus. Please help these people I'm praying for. Thank You for all You do and are. I praise You, Holy Spirit. Please fill me afresh. I worship You, Father. Please guide me in the way You want me to go.

Sometimes I use scripture in my prayers; sometimes I don't. But the bottom line is to focus on believing. Jesus said in the Gospel of John, "... This is the work (service) that God asks of you: that you believe in the One Whom He has sent" (John 6:29, AMPC).

I used to think that if I was eloquent, or prayed a long prayer, or threw in some impressive Bible verses (whether I actually believed them or not), then I was doing what God wanted. But God is way more interested in what is going on in my heart. He wants me to believe. He wants me to pray in faith on the basis of sincere trust. If I use scripture, He wants me to use the ones that are alive in my spirit and create faith in the hearing. He wants me to come to Him like a child—in healthy, trusting dependence. This is what He loves. And even though in many ways this seems too simple, I have come to appreciate the depth of His simplicity. His simplicity is profound.

There are also times when my prayers are more conversational. Even though He is already aware, I may want to tell God about something that just happened. Or get something uncomfortable "off my chest." There is relationship in the telling. This is what I do with my husband, my kids, and with my friends and family. I talk. Then I listen. This is what I try to do with God as well ... talk and listen. But I have to confess that I'm not always very good at listening. The truth is, it makes God's job a lot easier if I actually purpose to listen and trust that He has something to say. But I also know that God finds ways to talk to me whether I remember to listen or not. He's not above using unconventional means either. More than once, God has clearly spoken to me through a television commercial, mostly because, at the time, I was isolating, running away, and not listening to anything but the television. I have learned that God is persistent, creative, ingenious, practical, and personal. Even when you are running away, He will find you.

As for meditation, it simply means to reflect on the intended meaning of the author. Whether it's God speaking through His Word or another author speaking on recovery issues in a particular book, I can read and reflect on what the words mean to me and how I can apply them in my life. Application brings change, so that's a pretty important element too. But the reflection, or the meditating, is what seems to open the door of my mind and heart to the deeper meaning. There are so many ways to meditate. I can take one verse from Paul's epistles, or an entire Psalm of David, or a portion of the Proverbs, or a section of the Gospel of Mark or John, or a daily writing from a recovery book ... and just roll it around in my mind and work it. I look at it frontward, backward, and sideways, so to speak. I think about who the author is, what they are trying to say, and the real-life experience behind the written words. I look at it from different perspectives and sometimes imagine myself as a "player" in the scene. All of those reflections can shine a light on what's being said.

Sometimes I think about the emotions behind the words—like when Jesus is looking into the faces of those who keep demanding a sign because their hearts are filled with unbelief. Or when He locks His eyes with the Samaritan woman at the well after revealing the futility of her life story ... waiting to see if she will accept the Living Water that satisfies for all of eternity. Frankly, the more I allow myself to be visual and emotional, the more I see, and the stronger impact it creates. It helps me.

Sometimes I use a teaching resource to study the Word, or I let God reveal things to me as I'm journaling. At other times, I ask Him to show me His attributes as I read a portion of scripture. Those are some tools that work for me. But what works for you? How does God impact your heart?

All I know is that God isn't much into lifeless, religious forms that have no power. He's into what's real, true, and life changing. There are many, many tools that can be used on our "relationship journey" with God. As humans, we seem to instinctively choose the tools that speak to us the most and work for us the best.

Now, in the context of seeking a deeper walk with the Lord, the latter part of Step Eleven says to pray only for knowledge of His will for us and the power to carry that out. As I have mentioned, many years of my life were spent living my own way, even as a Christian. That doesn't mean I gave no thought to what God wanted, but it does mean that I was more preoccupied with survival and getting through the pain of each day than I was with the will of God. In fact, I had the attitude that the will of God was almost always going to be something I didn't want to do, like being a missionary in Africa or evangelizing on the streets of an inner city. Those are wonderful things but totally outside my comfort zone. So, back then, asking God to show me His will for my life seemed a little foolhardy. I was pretty certain I would end up being unhappy and forced to comply with an undesirable directive that was supposed to make me a better person.

Like I said … my attitude was in need of an overhaul.

I did not have a concept of God having my best interests at heart or really wanting good things for my life. Those concepts may have been in my head, but they were not "solid" in my heart. My underlying belief was that God was distant and generally unavailable to me. He took care of other people, but I was mostly on my own. He had lots of power, but I probably wouldn't see it in my life. And the good stuff happened to other people. So, praying for the knowledge of His will and the power to carry that out was not in my mental, emotional, or spiritual vocabulary.

Now, you may ask ... what changed?

What changed is that I hit bottom.

Then I genuinely gave my will and my life to God, holding nothing back. Somehow that seemed to open my heart to Truth. And that's the only way I know how to explain it. Where before, I was blind, I began to see much more clearly ... like adjusting the focus on a high-powered camera lens. Where before, I was bound, I started feeling free ... like stepping from a hot, stuffy house out into the cool, soft air of a new morning. Where before, I was powerless, I began to experience the ability to live my life without acting out addictively. And I knew it was God doing it because it sure wasn't me.

The Truth is: The divine empowerment to make right choices and live in God's way ... seems to come at the moment I surrender my desire and my need to live life my way. So, I believe that asking God to "show me His will and give me the power to carry it out" go hand in hand, one with the other. In my mind, that makes it pretty simple, and when "simple" comes from the heart of God, it works. This is a daily focus where I can get up each morning and, in faith, pray for the Lord to show me how He wants me to handle every situation and detail of my life. Every aspect. Every event. Every relationship. Every choice.

Then I defer to Him.

And the power comes.

This mode of operation makes each hour of each day uncomplicated, which is a good thing when your middle name used to be "Overanalytical." This is definitely a different focus for me, but in the Twelve Step program, most things fall under the category of *different*. And, out of necessity, I have built my relationship with God from a different standpoint. After decades of insanity, I was willing to do a lot of things differently. But, different or not, I have no doubt that God is truly the answer.

The *Big Book* says, "Remember that we deal with alcohol [or whatever your addiction is]—cunning, baffling, powerful! Without help it is too much for us. But there is One who has all power—that One is God. May you find Him now!"[35]

That is the essence of Step Eleven. This Step isn't recorded first or second in the list of Twelve Steps because a large number of folks just wouldn't be ready for it. By the time we actually get to this Step, there is a greater understanding of the utter importance and necessity of having the power and love of God in your life. And, by then, most of us have had the privilege of seeing God at work in our own lives and in the lives of others. That builds a mutual faith that is essential to recovery and contributes greatly to the relationships with others that are also vital to building a new life. And actually, it's just "cool" to watch God change other people at the same time He is changing me.

I was in a meeting not long ago, and a young man shared how he had wrestled with finding a new job. He had a family to support and was close to being desperate. And, like most of us, he had given much time and thought to fixing this problem. His efforts led him to conclude that a particular job, down to the last detail, would meet his family's need. However, when he pursued that avenue, the door slammed shut. That's where the rubber meets the road, and you find out what's really in your heart. And at that point, this man got on his knees and gave it up to the Lord. He gave up trying to make it happen; he gave up his personal plan; and he gave up his will. The next day, a thought came to him to apply at a different location, which he did, and within twenty-four hours, they called to offer him the job. Not only does this position provide for the financial needs of his family, but it's a good fit for their overall situation, and he loves the work. Loving your work is a nice little bonus.

It was all such a great testimony to the love, grace, and power of God.

That was a challenging experience for this young man, but as I watched God unveil the lesson and turn it into a huge blessing, it reminded me all over again that this Program is about learning to live successfully. And it's about discovering that God always has our best interests at heart. We have been called into a divinely designed relationship with the Almighty. So, I encourage you to "improve your conscious contact with God …"

… Then jump on the Potter's wheel and go for the ride of your life.

Step Twelve:
The Great Give-Away

WE HAVE FINALLY ARRIVED at the last of the Twelve Steps, but the unique thing about the Twelve Step program is that we never actually reach the end. This Program is a continuing circle of learning and growing that keeps on going and going and going. I'm sure there are those who would like to work through all of the Steps, receive a certificate of completion, and make their exit through the nearest door with a sigh of relief. But I have made peace with the knowledge that I will continue in this Program, in one way or another, for the rest of my life. And there are two very clear reasons why I hold that to be true: 1) I can't keep it unless I give it away; and 2) this is a new way of living ... a lifestyle that needs constant reinforcement.

Step Twelve says this: *Having had a spiritual awakening as the result of these Steps, we tried to carry this message to those still suffering and to practice these principles in all our affairs.*[36] Working through the Twelve Steps is supposed to lead us to a new place, spiritually, to make us aware of something we did not see before. Something that awakens us from a sleep-like state and stirs us into action, not only for ourselves, but for others. Whatever this something is, it's supposed to be so life changing, and so exciting, that we will want to share it with people we encounter on a daily basis. So, what is this mysterious awakening?

I can't speak for anyone else, so here's my take.

My world changed dramatically when I asked Jesus into my heart in 1975. It felt like "coming home." Although that was a long time ago, my commitment has not wavered because I'm much like the disciples who once said to Jesus, "Where else would we go?" I have never found anything or anyone who has even remotely touched my life in the way Jesus has. However, even though I made a commitment to live for God, I unknowingly tried to do that in my own strength and did not understand the great importance of surrendering my will, and every area of my life, to the only one who could empower me to walk in godliness—and that's God Himself. So, as a result, I tried to no avail to be "holy" on my own. There were certain things that changed and certain new habits that were formed, like going to church every Sunday and reading my Bible. But I never gained lasting victory over the sin and soul-sickness in my life—a fact which became a source of deep anguish.

Do you think I wanted to go out and shout from the rooftops how much I loved Jesus and tell everyone I met how much He had changed my life for the better? I did not. I lived in a state of frustration, coupled with the embarrassment and shame of falling so very short of what I thought were God's expectations. I couldn't put the food down. I lived with constant anxiety that I really wasn't aware of at the time. I didn't know what a healthy relationship looked like, and I carried resentments from the past. I also cultivated self-hatred, stayed in denial about the state of my first marriage for years, and fluctuated between controlling my kids and not being available to them while I acted out my addictions.

Simultaneously, I was going to church faithfully, studying the Bible diligently, praying for and serving others obediently, and worshipping God fervently. This was all very confusing. I had my public mask—and my hidden private life. I was tormented, split in two, and eventually began to fear for my salvation. I frankly wasn't sure where I would end up if I suddenly died. It was extremely obvious that there was still sin in my life, and when you don't understand the nature of grace—as was my predicament—you're left with nothing but condemnation. My sin spoke to me every day. And after many years, it screamed at me every day. I often hated my life. Do you really think I wanted to tell anyone about Jesus? I knew that He was good and His salvation was true, but my life was so far from what I thought it should be that I felt like my existence brought shame to the name of the Father. Part of the time, I just wanted to hide away in a closet with my bags of cheese puffs and boxes of donuts and not come out ... ever.

For some people in Twelve Step programs, the spiritual awakening unfolds over a certain season as they listen, learn, and grow. For others, it comes in the moment that they first believe in the existence of God.

My spiritual awakening came on the day that I finally acknowledged that nobody could manage my life successfully but Jesus. The day that I came to the end of myself, was the day I surrendered my whole life to God. He became "boss," and I resigned from trying to fill the position. At that point, I began to awaken to God and the things of God in a brand-new way. He has convicted me of every sinful choice I've made, and He has also faithfully guided me to sources of mental and emotional healing, which I gratefully received. He has allowed me to see, many times over, all the good that was accomplished by Him, in and through the years of struggle. They were not wasted years.

They have become part of my journey.

If every cloud (or hurricane) has a silver lining, the silver lining in this story is the extravagant, iridescent love of the Father God. My eyes have been opened. My heart has been filled. My soul is overflowing with gratitude. My love for Him abounds. There is no one like God. He alone deserves to sit on the Throne of Grace. His power is beyond comprehension. His wisdom is pure. His justice is true. And I have relationship with this wonderful Being because of the love and obedience of His perfect, blameless Son ... Jesus. My mission in this life is to share HIM. To become more and more like Him. To expound and teach on the awesomeness of His majesty. There is no higher purpose for me. If I can help just one person see who God really is, I will count myself a very happy human being.

This is my awakening.

This is something I can joyfully shout from the rooftops! I no longer feel like my existence is a black mark against God. I feel the warmth of His favor, His acceptance, and His approval. Those are sweet, sweet things that can't be bought with the riches of this world.

They can only be received as a gift from the heart of the Father—a gift that was purchased through the suffering, the death, and the resurrection of Jesus Himself.

Now, I wake up in the morning knowing that when God puts someone in my path, I will be able and willing to share the Good News with that person—because there really is good news! We are supposed to "carry this message to those still suffering" because there are thousands and millions of people who are still living in pain every day of their lives. They don't know the truth about God, about Jesus, or about themselves. So, as I'm willing to give away what I have been given, the offering becomes one of hope. And "telling" my story then comes full circle to reinforce a new way of life. The reminder of my past also places me in a posture of compassion toward those still struggling. I filled their shoes such a short time ago and don't ever want to forget that fact. I'm not interested in rehashing the pain just for the sake of going over it again, but I AM interested in sharing any experience, strength, and hope that might initiate a turning point for someone else. Besides, when I share what little I know, God has a tendency to bring more enlightenment. The blessings never really stop. I used to be caught up in a negative cycle that had no end, and now I'm caught up in a never-ending, positive cycle that goes on and on and on.

What's not to love about this Program and this life with God?

For those in recovery, having a message to share is a huge part of the healing.

It goes back to the importance of purpose, and when you're addicted, having real purpose gets syphoned out of your life. The months and years become progressively consumed with a self-focus that slowly obliterates anything as existential as purpose. Even if you once felt that you actually had a special reason to be alive, addiction has a way of suffocating and silencing the dream. It creeps in and literally takes you over in all the wrong ways. But recovery is largely about being "reborn" in certain respects and about finding restoration of things once lost. And, for some folks, sharing their recovery experience is the first real purpose they've ever had. It's a powerful thing to watch someone else being changed for the better, knowing that you've had a part in it. The transformation is from death to life. That's "God-territory." And, even though it's extremely obvious that God is the One doing the work, it's sweetly satisfying to know that we have been "tools in His hands" on occasion. It gives life a meaning that is unequaled by anything else.

Addiction has to be replaced. When you choose to let go of something that has been a huge "slice of the pie," you have to replace it with something equally as big. You can't just leave it void; it won't stay that way. And God knows that. How gracious and wise He is in giving us a new message and in allowing us to be an integral part of someone else's healing. This is big stuff.

So, we share our message. We share our experience, strength, and hope. And we watch God use it in whatever way He chooses. You may want to fasten your seat belt because He will surprise you with all the creative ways He reaches into the hearts and souls around you. I can recall a multitude of moments where, sitting in a Twelve Step meeting or getting together for coffee, I could "see" God moving in someone's life. You could see it in their faces, hear it in their words, feel it in their emotions, and witness it in their new choices.

A manifestation of liberty. Freedom found. What a monumental blessing this has been, and still is, to me. It fills me to the full, and that is God's masterful design.

When Jesus came to us, His creation, He chose a certain day and a certain message to announce His earthly ministry. That message is what we now know as Isaiah 61.

> "The Sovereign Lord has filled me with his Spirit.
> He has chosen me and sent me
> To bring good news to the poor,
> To heal the broken-hearted,
> To announce release to captives
> And freedom to those in prison.
> He has sent me to proclaim
> That the time has come
> When the Lord will save his people
> And defeat their enemies.
> He has sent me to comfort all who mourn,
> To give to those who mourn in Zion
> Joy and gladness instead of grief,
> A song of praise instead of sorrow.
> They will be like trees
> That the Lord himself has planted.
> They will all do what is right,
> And God will be praised for what he has done"
> (Isaiah 61:1–3, GNT).

The richness of those verses could span a lifetime. Do you hear the heart of God? Do you see His vision and the depth of His love? Do you hear His joy and expectation? It's all-encompassing, reaching into every facet of our lives. He is a complete God. He doesn't leave out anything. And that is paramount when you've been shackled by addiction. Those verses in Isaiah speak more to me now than they ever have. They are a promise of freedom, victory, joy, strength, purpose, and completeness. This is what Jesus chose to share as He launched His mission. And what a mission it was and still is! He lays out a choice in front of each one of us and says, "Here is life. I'm offering this life to you if you choose to receive."

I initially chose to receive in 1975. And thirty-eight years later, it culminated in putting my total trust in His divine love and authority. He put me in the right place at the right time to hear words that set me on fire with conviction and hope. And it was no small thing. To be set free from addiction is comparable to a blind man receiving his sight, a heart attack victim being revived, or a child, paralyzed from the waist, arising from a wheelchair to take steps on their own. Addiction is walking death. New life is a gift beyond expression. So, now, I have my own story to tell.

And *freedom* has become my message.

I think we all carry a core message exemplified in our day-to-day living. Something that, whether we realize it or not, becomes recognizable to others. Sometimes it's a good message, and sometimes it isn't.

"Trust in God."

"Be a rebel."

"Love conquers all."

"Money is everything."

"Giving is living."

For those recovering from addiction, the core message is that freedom is available. If you keep it to yourself, you lose it. If you give it away, it comes back to you. The sharing becomes a tool of recovery all by itself. That's why the *Big Book* is full of stories about men and women who found freedom through Twelve Step and continued in that freedom by helping others. The act is sometimes labeled as "paying it forward." But whichever way you choose to look at it, the principle is straightforward: if you've been given a great gift, pass it on to someone else. That's why I write about recovery. I want to keep the treasure of sobriety by sharing the "jewels."

I call it The Great Give-Away.

In a weekly Twelve Step group I attend, a new member recently joined our ranks. He's hungry for recovery and soaks it up like a sponge. He also shares his own experience, strength, and hope, and I am delighted by the fact that newcomers have the ability to inspire as much as anyone else. Sometimes more so. As I watch and listen to someone else traveling the road to freedom, maybe for the first time, I seem to relive the incredible freshness of liberation. My own commitment and excitement are renewed, and life takes on a deeper joy and greater satisfaction. I think we feel something akin to that when we see a newborn baby. Our perspective of life is renewed in the potential and hope of wonderful things to come for that child. There is just an innate happiness that envelops us when we see the work of God's hands, a brand-new baby created by His heart of love. "Newcomers" carry a similar potential and hope. We rejoice in their courage to begin a journey into the unknown, and we only want to encourage and strengthen their resolve to discover a different way to live and a brighter future to share.

Their presence is life-giving. Literally.

And there's more.

One of our goals in recovery is to primarily become a better person and grow out of the character defects that contributed to, or were created by, the sin and sickness that dominated our lives. Addiction is characterized by tunnel vision, self-pity, resentment, and gross negativity, "crowned" by self-centeredness. But the opposite of being self-centered is being "others-centered."

In the *Big Book*, there's a story of a recovering alcoholic who, after six months of sobriety, almost gave in to the "first drink" while on an out-of-town business trip. A lucrative deal that would have set him up financially fell through in a big way. He was devastated. Alone, and under great mental and emotional pressure, he knew that his only salvation lay in reaching out to another human being suffering from alcoholism. He called a church, was directed to a local man with such a condition, and made arrangements to visit the man and tell his story. With the decision to be "others-centered," the urge to take the first drink lifted off of him immediately. That businessman was Bill Wilson, and the man he visited that night was Dr. Bob who, shortly thereafter, found his own sobriety. The two later became the founders of Alcoholics Anonymous.[37]

There are times when giving of yourself becomes the panacea of the moment. Temptation falls away, negativity turns to joy, or a downcast spirit becomes rejuvenated. I experience this frequently in Twelve Step meetings. My thoughts and emotions become others-centered through sharing some portion of my story and giving away something that has become a part of me. Instead of being a taker, I become a giver. And that creates unity with the character of God, the One who gave His only Son to die for us. It's also a relationship builder. And because God is so very relational, He is pleased by the caring and compassion manifested in the act. Overall, it demonstrates the fact that stepping into agreement with God connects us with love, strength, and power. It is truly "more blessed to give than to receive" (Acts 20:35, NLT).

The proof is in the pudding.

Offering the Message of Life to someone who is addicted is like throwing a life preserver to someone drowning in the sea. God is the One true Liberator, but He uses many tools in the process, including those of us in recovery. When I share my message of freedom, I'm ultimately sharing God. And He is the power source. I have come to believe that, apart from Him, there is no freedom.

And in God's world, giving away what you have never decreases the supply—it only multiplies the gift.

Now the last part of Step Twelve talks about the practice of these principles. We've all heard the cliché that "practice makes perfect." And even though we are striving more for progress than perfection in our recovery, there is much value in the principle of repetition. If you keep doing something over and over again, usually you get pretty good at it. This Program is no different. We've talked before about this being a process that involves a series of gradual changes, and that's why lasting recovery actually manifests itself in a new lifestyle. It's not a six- or twelve-month class that I take in order to acquire a certain number of educational credits. To me, recovery is living life on God's pathway. A pathway that works. There are certain guidelines that we are to follow, such as walking in humility, learning to trust, letting God be God, self-examination, bravely admitting our weaknesses and mistakes, and asking for help. Then we are to submit to positive change, right our wrongs, forgive offenses, release pain, stay diligent, keep growing with God, and share our stories to help others as we continue practicing our new way of life.

These are the fundamentals that consistently guide us to healing. And they have to be diligently reinforced to avoid falling back into old patterns. I can veer off course and default into those old ways, but as I recognize what has happened, I can get right back on the "straight and narrow," so to speak. This is a raised highway—a road not taken by all because it's not easy. But the benefits are boundless.

Here's what the *Big Book of Alcoholics Anonymous* says about those benefits: "If we are painstaking about this phase of our development, we will be amazed before we are half way through. We are going to know a new freedom and a new happiness. We will not regret the past nor wish to shut the door on it. We will comprehend the word serenity and we will know peace. No matter how far down the scale we have gone, we will see how our experience can benefit others. That feeling of uselessness and self-pity will disappear. We will lose interest in selfish things and gain interest in our fellows. Self-seeking will slip away. Our whole attitude and outlook upon life will change. Fear of people and of economic insecurity will leave us. We will intuitively know how to handle situations which used to baffle us. We will suddenly realize that God is doing for us what we could not do for ourselves."[38]

In Twelve Step circles, those phrases are affectionately called "The Promises." They are the promises of the Program if you work the Steps ... but only if you work the Steps.

James 1: 22–25 says it way better than I ever could: "And remember, it is a message to obey, not just to listen to. So don't fool yourselves. For if a person just listens and doesn't obey, he is like a man looking at his face in a mirror; as soon as he walks away, he can't see himself anymore or remember what he looks like. But if anyone keeps looking steadily into God's law for free men, he will not only remember it but he will do what it says, and God will greatly bless him in everything he does (James 1:22–25, TLB).

In 1991, when my Heavenly Father began a long season of healing in my life, I knew it would be life changing. And it has been. I'm on a journey, and the journey no longer has a destination. It has simply become the life that I am living, and I wouldn't trade it for anything.

My prayer for all of us, right now, is that we would each step forward into our healing journeys. That we would "be strong and courageous and get to work" (1 Chronicles 28:20, TLB). I can't promise you that it will be painless and without struggle. But I can promise that the end result will be worth any pain that is endured. In fact, it will be exhilarating. And we will never be alone in the journey, for God is our partner, and so is every other person on the pathway of recovery.

The Twelve Steps are stepping-stones of promise that lead to freedom, strength, and great joy. May you embrace them with your whole heart and commit to the godly principles that are held within. They have worked for me; they have worked for many others; and they will work for YOU

... If you work them.

God's greatest blessings to you always.

Break it Down

THE TWELVE STEP PROGRAM has a lot of slogans. I suppose that's because they're catchy and easy to remember ... phrases like "easy does it," "live and let live," "first things first," and "turn it over." If you go to Twelve Step meetings, you'll hear these slogans verbalized frequently and will begin to understand what they actually mean in the context of recovery. I have been in many situations where the pressure was on. I needed to make a choice, and for the life of me, I couldn't put two sensible words together in my head. That can happen when I'm tired, afraid, or angry. But, thankfully, a Twelve Step slogan often pops into my head and brings some semblance of rational thinking to the forefront. Sometimes, they are lifesavers. I don't know for sure how they pop into my head, but as they say, "don't look a gift horse in the mouth." I choose not to analyze it too much. One of the slogans that has been particularly helpful for me is "one day at a time."[39] Those words have become very familiar and often keep me anchored in the Land of Sanity.

When I made the choice to turn my will and my life over to God, I discovered that there were many components to recovery. There was no question that I needed to stop bingeing, stop trying to control others, and learn to have a healthy dependence on God. But living life was like groping around in a thick fog, constantly searching for something that looked familiar or felt comfortable. The problem was: a lot that was familiar and comfortable to me was dysfunctional. It just didn't work.

Let me be the first to say that this realization was completely overwhelming! In the days of addiction, I lived from one anxiety to the next, from one binge to the next, and from one negative situation to the next. How was I supposed to change all that? I had never possessed the ability or strength to do that on my own. Every time I thought about not bingeing for the rest of my life, I would feel panic rise up on the inside of me, threatening to cut off my air supply. And that was closely followed by the sensation of a brick dropping into the pit of my stomach ... because I knew I would fail. Actually, there was a season when the thought of really turning my life over to God created the same reaction. But I had reached a point where staying the same was not an option. I couldn't stand the thought of it. I had to move forward. I had to change.

As I started the healing journey, one of my biggest challenges was learning to trust myself. I can't tell you how many times I made a solemn promise to God to never binge again ... and did. It happened over and over again. So, trusting myself to make any kind of commitment, and keep it, became a moot point. I learned to avoid doing such things. But as I attended Twelve Step meetings and listened to the stories of others who were being set free, I kept hearing the phrase:

"One Day at a Time." And, as with many aspects of the Program, I eventually came to understand what that motto means for a recovering addict.

The first part has to do with breaking down my commitment to sobriety into segments of time that seem manageable. It's always in God's strength, but it feels much easier to say, "Okay, God, for the next twenty-four hours I choose to live binge free," instead of saying, "I'll never binge again for the rest of my life." I can't wrap my brain around "the rest of my life," but committing to a twenty-four-hour segment seems workable in comparison. There are many times when I find myself saying this in the morning during my quiet time, and it helps. I can set my mind and heart on that goal and have a reasonable amount of confidence that it will be accomplished.

Or, when breaking things down, how about this? Today, I choose to be happy, have a good attitude, be productive, and not criticize anyone. Now, there's a list to tackle one day at a time! The overall concept is to have a positive frame of mind—but I mention those four things because they are often a challenge for recovering addicts. And for me, especially the part about not criticizing. Oftentimes, we end up dishing out what we heard and experienced as children, even when we swear up and down that we won't. We repeat the scenario.

At one time or another, with certain people in my sphere, I have played the broken record with the same 'ole tune. Critical words. Words to try to "influence" someone else's choice or decision. Words that are intended to motivate but actually flow from a desire to control. Words not especially meant to be unkind but which carry a negative content.

Some time ago, I had to once again face this character defect in regard to my husband. I found myself mentioning how he could comb his hair differently, how many hours he had been looking at social media that evening, how the trash bag was still sitting in the garage, and "aren't those jeans getting too tight"? He finally brought it to my attention and pointed out the trend my words were taking. Up until then, I didn't even see it for what it was. Faultfinding. In my mind, he wasn't doing it my way, or the way I thought was best, or the way he surely would agree with if I just shared my opinion.

Oh, brother.

When I tried to stop, I found out how automatically my mind goes there. So, the faultfinding, critical words became a focus for prayer, and I quickly realized that I needed to apply the "one day at a time" concept to this problem. God and I needed to work on it together. And, thankfully, the same principle holds true: when I break those things down into one-day commitments, they are more doable, and I somehow have the faith to believe that God will get me through. And on the days that I need to break down a commitment into one hour, or even into five minutes, that's okay. I'm just trying to do whatever I can to keep myself focused on submitting my will and trusting God.

"One day at a time" can be a pivotal thought that changes the course of my day. And I understand a little better now when someone says, "I've put a few 'twenty-fours' together, and it's turning out pretty well." When those consecutive days build to a place where I'm riding a wave of recovery on the surfboard of God's power . . . it feels mighty good.

The second meaning of "one day at a time" has to do with focus. In the past, my thoughts and feelings were all over the place like shot from a scattergun. I was consumed with negative memories of what I had already done or by anxiety over what was coming ahead that I might not know how to handle. Believe me, there is no quicker way to have a miserable life. Living in the moment and making something intentionally good out of today wasn't something that I practiced. But "one day at a time" provides me with a mental shift. It gives me a new perspective. And I have found, that from the moment I choose to change my focus, God empowers me to live that way.

This can become very important in the Land of Recovery. I have listened to testimonies of enough Twelve Steppers to know that regret over the past is a common malady. Let's face it. We've all done some pretty lousy things and made some pretty lousy choices—things that were hurtful, harmful, and destructive toward others and ourselves. So, we have a tendency to feel bad. We also have a tendency to feel ashamed, guilty, and depressed when we think about it. And if you spend a lot of time thinking about it, you get the expected results.

One of the high priorities in recovery is to put the past to rest. And that's a good way to say it: put it to rest. Our memories can be irritatingly active, with all the previous emotions attached. At any moment of the day, or in wakeful hours of the night, the thoughts can move in like a tornadic wall cloud or crash down the door of your mind like a Viking warrior. They can bring heaviness, sadness, and torment, along with an ache in the pit of your stomach. So, we work on those Steps that help us deal with what *was*—in order to enjoy what *is*. That doesn't mean we forget what happened because we hope to learn from our history and steer clear of repetitions. But it does mean that we do all we know to do to resolve the situation. We admit it, confess it, ask God to change us, forgive, ask forgiveness, deal with the pain, make amends, and then let it go. If we can't let it go, our hearts are usually trying to tell us something. That's when we may need to find a counselor who can guide us through the healing we need to receive from God for that particular situation.

That's how we find rest.

For a long time, I didn't know you could remember painful events in vivid detail *without* feeling the emotions all over again. Life has taught me that if the memories aren't healed, the emotions are still intact, even though I may deny them or stuff them. But healing brings release. It releases the pain and enables me to remember without experiencing "the emotional reruns." On occasion, a stubborn memory may try to resurrect a dark wave of guilt, rejection, shame, or regret. So, I have also learned to talk to myself.

"It is what it is."

"The past is the past."

"I've done what I need to do."

"Continuing in shame and guilt serves no purpose whatsoever."

"Let it go."

Talking to myself helps. It can reset my posture, my stance, my emotions, and my attitude. That can be extremely valuable. And don't underestimate the power of God to assist you in your efforts. I have called upon Him many times to help change the flow of my mental/emotional trend, and He has done just that. Then, after thirty minutes, I may pause and realize that the "harassment" has stopped, and my frame of mind has completely changed. If you don't think that's a blessing... just try it.

Keeping things manageable and focused goes a long way toward living each day in peace. And living in peace largely comes from reminding myself that I have turned my life over to God's care. There isn't one detail that slips by Him. He is thoughtful and vigilant. My prayer is that one day, if you don't know already, you will come to understand the depth of God's love and the completeness of His provision for you. He has an amazing ability to "read" your heart and meet your needs because He is your Creator. So, be confident in that knowledge and choose to believe that you can handle life.

... One day at a time.

Steps One, Two, and Three
... the ER of Recovery

WHEN I FIRST STARTED IN RECOVERY, learning how to apply the Steps to my own personal life was a primary goal. Decades of addiction had worn me down, leaving me exhausted and ill in more ways than one. The book of Proverbs says that "hope deferred makes the heart sick" (Proverbs 13:12, TLB), and that's the state I was in on the day of my first AA meeting. Desperate to learn, I was excited to find out that anyone could get a free education at Twelve Step meetings just by showing up and listening. Almost everyone had good things to say, but I quickly learned to pay special attention when the "veterans" spoke at our meetings. They had long-term sobriety, the time-tested wisdom to go with it, and a wonderful willingness to share what they had experienced. So, it wasn't long before I started hearing about "applying the first three Steps." The explanation was easy to understand, and since I was ready to try all suggestions, I started using this recovery tool in my own life to see what would happen.

I was not disappointed with the results.

Let me begin by reviewing the first three Steps:

1. Admitted we were powerless over (fill in the blank with your addiction or affliction), and that our lives had become unmanageable.
2. Came to believe that a Power greater than ourselves could restore us to sanity.
3. Made a decision to turn our will and our lives over to the care of God as we understood Him.[40]

Some Program "old-timers" summarize those first three Steps with the words: I can't. God can. I think I'll let Him. So, I began to repeat that phrase to myself, "I can't. God can. I think I'll let Him." Somehow it gave me comfort to say it. It gave me an increasing sense that I was, indeed, going to be okay. That I wouldn't be stuck in squalor for the rest of my life and die with the millstone of addiction around my neck. It was like a breath of fresh air after a carbon dioxide overload. In the months that followed, I started using that phrase in situations that were making me feel crazy, and it always led to better ground. It still does. And after all the intellectual analyzing I had done over the years in an effort to beat this thing on my own, this uncomplicated approach was a delight.

I started using food to push down my feelings somewhere around the age of three. So, by the time I was fifty-nine, I was well practiced in that unhealthy habit, which had long since turned into an addiction primarily fueled by deep insecurity, depression, self-pity, self-centeredness, and a boatload of fear. In addition to that, I was overly dependent, controlling, had social anxiety, and was a people pleaser, which often led to resentment and anger. When you need the approval of others to feel good about yourself, you are constantly agreeing to do what you really don't want to do in order to win the "prize." I had lots of negativity rolling around inside. Food bingeing covered up a lot of those emotions when they surfaced, which happened frequently, but it sure didn't make the emotions disappear.

When I finally chose the Twelve Step program and abstinence, and no longer had the food bingeing to help me cope with life, I needed some answers. My thoughts and feelings were still driving me nuts. Circumstances were driving me nuts. Other people were driving me nuts. Loneliness and depression were driving me nuts. Well ... you get the picture. Even though I was trying really hard to walk with God and do what was right, insanity lurked around every corner.

I had a lot to learn.

The really great thing about not bingeing is that active submission to God somehow causes your eyes to be opened to troublesome issues. When we're still blind to a problem, we can't do anything about it. But when we see it, God gives us the power to deal with it. Thankfully, I started seeing three big culprits all at about the same time: my lack of trust, my negativity, and my outside focus. And that's when I started learning how to use Steps One, Two, and Three in very practical ways.

I used to torment myself during the Christmas holiday season due to my perfectionism. It takes an incredible amount of energy and effort to be "perfect." On a particular occasion, I felt resentful and completely overwhelmed by how much I had to get done on a specific day, as well as the next few days after that. The operative word here is overwhelmed. As panic started rising up inside and tears began to fill my eyes, I recognized that I had crossed over into an old, familiar area of "insanity." I knew I wasn't trusting God. So, I took the situation to Him in prayer and applied the first Three Steps. I was honestly powerless over how I was feeling at that moment, and my life felt very unmanageable—so I confessed that. Then I chose to believe that in those circumstances, God could restore me to a place of sanity where I could see new choices and options that would lead to a place of peace instead of panic.

As I turned it all over to God, putting my life in His hands, He showed me exactly what to do. It just floated up from the inside, and I carried out the instructions that I was hearing. The panic totally left, and the day turned out to be productive and successful. The next day, however, I felt exhausted physically and emotionally. Thankfully, God sent a good friend to encourage me to take the afternoon to regenerate myself, which I chose to do. And, as I trusted the Lord to help me finish my work in the remaining available time, He was faithful to do just that.

Eureka!

In my old life, I would have panicked. I would have been angry. I would have resentfully done the whole work list without asking for any help and then I would have rewarded myself with a huge binge at the first opportunity. That's a classic example of "insanity." It's a way of approaching life that doesn't work. And that kind of insanity can manifest in many different ways, such as: giving in to all kinds of fear, confusion about why I'm upset, resentment over circumstances out of my control, wanting to hang on to unforgiveness, unrighteous anger toward others, and hearing someone's innocent comments through the filter of insecurity and low self-esteem—just to name a few. These are all pesky rascals. But applying Steps One, Two, and Three to deal with any of these obstacles can bring new focus and immediate relief.

I can't. God can. I think I'll let Him.

The other key factor in all of this is God's power. It's easy to underestimate the supernatural element of the Twelve Step program, but when we choose to live God's way, He is very invested in giving us the power to do so. When I apply the first three Steps to a challenging situation, it somehow ushers in an assistance that often goes beyond natural explanation. This is especially noticeable to me when I'm dealing with relationships.

The other day, I felt impressed to give some written materials to a person who is a brand-new Christian and on the cusp of entering recovery. For particular reasons, I needed to enlist the help of my husband in order to do so. He suggested one way of getting the material to the person, and I suggested another way that seemed easier and more logical in my mind. He did not agree.

... Do you see the red flag waving?

Such simple things can wreak havoc in relationships when one or both of you have the need to control. Ever been there? I felt the flash of irritation when he didn't automatically yield to my logic and immediately recognized my desire to be in control. The recognition, in itself, was a miracle. One of the great benefits of recovery is identifying "button-pushers." Another powerful benefit is learning to handle button-pushers in ways that work.

Previously, this kind of situation would have felt unmanageable, and my need to control would have pushed me into that realm of insanity where there is "only one way to do things." My way. In years past, I can remember feeling this vague, nagging fear—that if things weren't done in the way I thought was best, then something would go wrong. All of which often led to conflict and upset. But I am practicing new ways of approaching these relationship dynamics. So, I silently prayed a short prayer and turned it over to God. I let go of my need to control. And I asked God to work it out in the way He knew was best for all concerned. God's way, not mine. As it turned out, in that particular situation, my husband ended up delivering the materials in the way I had suggested, but it wasn't because I pushed him or insisted. That doesn't work with my husband—or with the great majority of men that I know. Nor should it. I didn't say one more word about it. Not when he argued and not when he ended up going along with my suggestion. The materials were delivered, and we stayed in peace with each other.

Now, I shared that to say that there was one specific moment when I felt the power of God working on my behalf. I could almost physically feel it kick in. Can you guess when it happened? Yep. When I gave up the desire to be in control. In a flash of revelation, my "insanity" was exposed, and God offered me a better option. When I chose to let go, this sweet peace came up on the inside and settled in my soul. Even if my husband had made a different choice, the peace would have remained. I was trusting God.

That's what I'm talking about when I say that God empowers us to do His will. This same kind of thing happens to me in many different areas of life. And how grateful I am.

I like this new way much better.

Now, why do I call this the ER of Recovery? The Emergency Room is where primary, essential care is given. That which is needed first. In many, if not all recovery situations, the first thing we need is humility, healthy dependence, and the determination to handle life God's way. That's the foundation from which we launch all other actions and efforts. Steps One, Two, and Three are crucial for centering ourselves in the kind of balance that leads to sanity ... living life with a faith that works. I've been practicing this tool long enough now that it has become largely automatic. I can assess the circumstances, apply the primary care to get through the rough place, and then follow up with detailed care as time, knowledge, and provisions allow.

You will soon discover, as I did, that there are lots of opportunities to get this right.

Just as I was finishing breakfast one morning, our cat, who is disgustingly cute, knocked over one of our big, potted plants. He was climbing where he should not have been and accidentally pushed it off of the fireplace mantle. The pot broke, dirt spewed everywhere, and the plant lay on the floor, roots naked and exposed. I was not happy. Neither was our cat when I banished him to the bedroom. I knew it was going to take over an hour to clean up the mess, and as I retrieved the vacuum, I started grumbling to myself. Admittedly, the grousing went on for about ten minutes as I tried to think of a way to rein in an unruly six-month-old "kitten." To no avail. In the midst of my irritation and frustration, the sarcastic thought came that I should just have a binge and turn the whole day into a disaster, since we were off to such a "good start."

A typical old tape.

Well, I caught that thought immediately and reminded myself that I was committed to living life with God's help—and without using excess food. I also reminded myself that emotions are temporal. And fickle. They can change in a moment of time. As I gave it all to God, the temptation lifted immediately, as well as the irritation. Truthfully, I needed to clean the living room anyway, and this mess just helped me get past the procrastination.

The lesson was reinforced again. I can handle life as I trust in the Lord's care, His goodness, and His power.

So can you.

I dare you to try it.

Forgiveness ...
Release and Relief

IN ALL HONESTY, there are few things that I have come across in life that meet more resistance than the act of forgiving those who have hurt us. I have gone through my own struggles and have witnessed a multitude of others who either worked through their resistance or have suffered by clinging to their pain. Forgiveness can sometimes be a bit complicated, and Jesus has a lot to say on this subject, so it becomes a topic that should be examined carefully. I have always believed that if Jesus mentioned something more than once, He did so because He knew how important it was. Or He knew how hard it was going to be, at times, for us to obey.

If you've been hanging on to unforgiveness for weeks, or months, or years, let me ask you a simple question ...

Are you finding that to be helpful?

I'm extremely grateful that, as a young believer, I received a good amount of teaching on forgiveness. If I hadn't, I don't even want to think about where I might be right now. The teaching has given me solid motivation to forgive, even when it's hard to do so. It has continued to bring godly conviction that has lasted for decades. But this has not been an easy process, and there has been much to learn through practical experience, enlightened by God's wisdom.

I was saved in 1975 when I was twenty years old. At that time, I still carried the pain from the childhood difficulties and challenges that had occurred. I did not have a good relationship with my parents. My dad was into full-blown alcoholism in those years, and I was still struggling with the perception of my mom being distant and critical. I did not know how to forgive them, compounded by the fact that living with them often led to the emotional wounds being repeatedly reopened. The first summer that I was saved, I made my new faith known to my parents, getting a bare acknowledgment from my dad and actual persecution from my mom. She was openly hostile and made cutting remarks about my Christianity. She doesn't do that anymore, thank goodness, but at the time, it was a painful continuation of what had always felt like open rejection from her. When I started learning about forgiveness and realized I needed to extend grace to my parents, I did the best I could. But I couldn't seem to get rid of the resentment toward them. The hurt went deep, and they weren't showing any signs of altering their behavior. The unfortunate thing is: my behavior toward *them* wasn't much better, and because of that, I don't think my Christianity made much of a positive impression.

I struggled for another ten years before the breakthrough started coming—a change which primarily occurred due to three specific reasons: 1) I started letting God make genuine changes in *me*; 2) I started taking responsibility for *my* part in the relationship; and 3) I gained a new perspective of my parents and a compassion toward them through counseling. That last one made a big difference. I began to see life through their eyes, asking myself and God why they made the choices they made. When the questions started getting answered, the resentment began to melt away.

Two things were learned from that counseling experience. One is that it really does help to "walk in the other person's shoes." Sometimes it only takes a brief moment of identifying with the other person's pain to receive the gift of "new eyes." Secondly, those who are emotionally broken and struggling with pain often end up bestowing pain on others. That was true for my parents, and it has been true of me. When I saw the humanness of my parents and stopped villainizing them, it was much easier to forgive. In addition, the fact that God was healing *my* heart at the same time became a significant factor in the process.

There is something uniquely supernatural that happens when God heals our hearts. If you have never experienced this, I pray that you *will* very soon because our God is an amazing God. His heart of love toward us is beyond our farthest and deepest imagination. His desire to heal us and make us whole goes to the very core of His being—so much so that He gave His only Son to die for that cause. Love heals. Love is the most powerful force in the universe. And what happens when God heals your heart, is that His LOVE covers the transgression and washes away the pain. It is an unforgettable, divine work of the Holy Spirit.

And oftentimes, *choosing* to forgive sets that love into motion.

One of the best things I ever heard about forgiveness is that it begins as a choice. A choice made apart from my feelings and emotions. If I wait for my feelings to get all warm and fuzzy toward the person I need to forgive, I'll probably never get there. I was taught that if I choose to let go of the offense as an act of my will, then God will honor my obedience by giving me the right feelings and emotions to go with it. That's the power of love in operation. Sometimes, I have to take a stand in faith, reminding myself that I have made the choice to forgive. But when I do that, God helps me release the negative emotions and come to a place of peace, especially when I pray sincerely for the person who has hurt or offended me.

Something else that helped me choose to forgive was having a better understanding of how important forgiveness is to God.

John's Gospel says, "For God loved the world so much that he gave his only Son so that anyone who believes in him shall not perish but have eternal life" (John 3:16, TLB).

That's one of those power-packed scriptures that reveals the incredible depth of His compassion. And it helps to read between the lines. Before believing in Jesus, I was headed toward death and a separation from God that would last for eternity. Sin was the "separator," and God's forgiveness of that sin was the only way to change my trajectory. But a price had to be paid to obtain that forgiveness, so God sent Jesus to pay it. The perfect, sinless blood of Jesus was poured out on God's altar to pay the price for my sin. So, because God gave what was most precious to Him in order to legally appropriate forgiveness for me, my unforgiveness toward others can become a denial of God's grace and a denial of His gift. Forgiveness is what He offers to me so that I can come into His presence and live with Him forever. If I refuse to give to *others* the same forgiveness that was so very costly for God to give to *me*, then I can place myself in a precarious position.

As Jesus prayed The Lord's Prayer, He said, "Give us today the food we need, and forgive us our sins, as we have forgiven those who sin against us. And don't let us yield to temptation, but rescue us from the evil one. If you forgive those who sin against you, your heavenly Father will forgive you. But if you refuse to forgive others, your Father will not forgive your sins" (Matthew 6:11–15, NLT).

In *The Message Bible,* those same verses read, "Keep us alive with three square meals. Keep us forgiven with You and forgiving others. Keep us safe from ourselves and the Devil. You're in charge!" [Jesus goes on to say ...] "In prayer there is a connection between what God does and what you do. You can't get forgiveness from God, for instance, without also forgiving others. If you refuse to do your part, you cut yourself off from God's part" (Matthew 6:11-15, MSG).

That's a good way to think about it ... you cut yourself off from God's part.

There are certain Biblical teachings or principles that carry a *spiritual force*, meaning the principle itself originated in God's world, and the impact goes beyond the natural world that we can see. Love is one of those teachings. Since God IS love, it's easy to see how love is a supernatural force. Covenants fall in that category as well. We live by the teachings of the Old and New Covenants, which obviously carry eternal power and significance in the spirit realm.

There is also a spiritual force tied to forgiveness.

Forgiveness connects me with God, with His power, with His love, with His freedom, and with His protection. Those are big, big things that can make a huge difference in my life. But without that spiritual enlightenment, the benefits of forgiveness can be easy to overlook and hard to comprehend. By knowingly or unknowingly holding unforgiveness in my heart, I may actually be walking away from God's power, love, freedom, and protection—and suffering the consequences thereof.

... So, why do we hang on to something that's not good, and even destructive?

I used to hold on to unforgiveness because I thought somehow it would protect me from getting hurt again, especially by that same person and in the same way. That may not have been a conscious thought, but it was there underneath the surface. I was afraid, and unforgiveness was my perceived wall of safety. It was a wall that I thought would keep out pain, but instead, it ended up holding me captive. There have been painful situations in my life where unforgiveness seemed like a reasonable choice, but ultimately, it became a huge black hole.

I also used to linger in unforgiveness because I thought I would be *condoning* the other person's actions and behaviors if I forgave them and let it go. At some point, I realized that this was an inaccurate belief. The message carried in God's forgiveness toward us has never included a declaration that our sin is okay; He just declares His willingness to not hold it against us. He chooses to cover that sin with His love. Our forgiveness of someone's hurtful, unjust actions toward us is not a declaration of absolution. We are not saying that it's okay. But we *are* declaring that covering the sin with the love of God is a better way, and a more profitable way, especially for us. The day that I really understood that my choice to forgive was the best choice for *me* ... was the day that I became more willing to cooperate. That sounds a little selfish, but it's actually the truth.

I also had to realize that part of this process involves *healthy boundaries*. Just because I forgive someone doesn't mean I have to go back and let them hurt me again. God gives me wisdom about the people I choose to be around, how often, and in what capacity. I can forgive someone and purpose to love them without making myself vulnerable to their continuing abuse or mistreatment. A healthy boundary sets up parameters in which to operate safely. So, if I have questions about what is or isn't healthy, I can seek wise input from my sponsor, trusted friends, and God.

Thankfully, we are not alone in this. Help is available. And that's a good thing because I am not Superwoman. Some offenses are smaller and less significant, and I can forgive "on my own," so to speak. But there are times when the act of forgiveness can only be accomplished with the help of God, especially in those times when I don't even have the willingness to try. If that's the case, I know I can pray for that very thing. Willingness. If I ask sincerely, God will give it to me, and the rest will follow. The good news is: no matter how long I carry unforgiveness in my heart, God always shows up with supernatural assistance when I choose to do things His way.

In the end, I finally realized that forgiveness takes me on a fast track back to the big T-word: TRUST. I am amazed at how often the Steps and principles of recovery come back around to that same component. In the past, I spent an incredible amount of time and effort trying to control *things*, and *people*, and *events*—instead of trusting my life to God. And my unforgiveness was indicative of me trying to run my world. But after forty years of addiction, I decided that my way of running the world wasn't working very well, and I started learning how to let God be in charge. He does it so much better. I can trust Him to be the God of justice and fairness that His Word declares Him to be. I can trust Him to "have my back." I can put my desire for revenge into His hands, and let it go. I can choose to let His love cover all transgressions, which keeps me in a place of rest and contentment.

Trusting Him will accomplish all of that.

There are some very wise words in *The Message Bible* that are worth remembering: "Be even-tempered, content with second place, quick to forgive an offense. Forgive as quickly and completely as the Master forgave you. And regardless of what else you put on, wear love. It's your basic, all-purpose garment. Never be without it" (Colossians 3:13-14, MSG).

Love is a powerful force. God's love leads to forgiveness.

May you find it now.

The Power of Our Story

TWELVE STEP SUPPORT GROUPS are invaluable when they fulfill their original purpose, which is to *carry a message of recovery* to those seeking freedom from addiction. Recovery is definitely a choice and will always be available to those who are ready to receive it, but a good support group can be an instrument in the hands of God to help a hurting heart become ready for that change.

Most people who walk into a Twelve Step meeting are looking for a better way to live life because on some level, they have acknowledged that they're not functioning well. When those people finally get the courage to come to a meeting, hearing words of recovery can provide practical experience, tangible strength, and life-changing hope. A lot of people who walk through that door for the first time are barely hanging on by a thread. So, finding hope is essential. I don't know about you, but I won't try *anything* unless I have a reasonable amount of hope that it's going to work! And hope is exactly what I found one day as I sat in a Twelve Step support group meeting.

I really didn't know what to expect that Saturday morning when God guided me into an AA meeting. It was my first experience with this particular group. They opened with a moment of silence followed by the three-line Serenity Prayer. And as everyone said that simple prayer in unison, I suddenly knew, instinctively, that I was no longer alone. I was surrounded by voices—by people—who knew my pain. They knew my thoughts, had felt my feelings, and had lived my life in one way or another. I started choking back tears right then and there because I had spent my whole life feeling inadequate, feeling different, and feeling alone. The sense of physical relief that washed over me was like a rope thrown to someone mired in quicksand. I sat there, quietly crying through most of that meeting, because I knew that my life had just changed in an unspoken and inexplicable way. I found great hope and courage in the words that were shared.

It's important to understand that what gave me hope that morning was what I heard, and by the grace of God, I was ready to hear exactly what He wanted me to hear. I listened to one person after another share how miserable and painful their lives had been. Some had grown up with an alcoholic parent, much like I had; some had been temporarily successful in life or business; some had been in and out of jail; and some had been close to death. But all who shared that day ended with a similar expression of gratitude for the freedom they were finding. They thanked God and the principles of the Twelve Steps for their freedom. Many confessed that they didn't know God at all when they first arrived, but God found them as they began working the Program. They had come to understand that the recovery principles are God directed and God inspired—that the Steps actually lead to God and to freedom. Whether it was audibly spoken, or just implied between the lines, I heard over and over again, "God did this for me, and God will do it for you."

I got the message.

Or, as some folks in the Program say, "The message got me." Others say that recovery isn't something that is understood intellectually; it is "caught" by faith as we listen with our hearts to those who are experiencing freedom. There does seem to be a transfer of faith, or osmosis of some kind, as you listen to others share their stories. That's the God part. Seeing and hearing how God and His Steps are successfully working in the lives of others has a tendency to empower us with the courage to begin the process ourselves.

However, once we begin the process, we discover the need for a certain kind of strength that we did not have before. The first Step of recovery invites us to admit our powerlessness, which necessitates connecting with a new strength that will help us change our course. God Himself is the first and foremost component of that strength, and we gain that strength by surrendering all to Him. That's why Old-Timers in the Program will tell you that dependency on God and walking in humility are the way to make progress. Most of us walked into Twelve Step thinking that the only one we could rely upon was ourselves. But that turned out to be problematic ... since we finally had to admit that our own strength wasn't enough.

The concept of depending on God, and others, is often very foreign. We don't know how to do it. We don't know if we want to do it. We're scared to even try. But what choice do we have if we want to get better? We find strength when we hear the stories of others who repeatedly tell us that God can be trusted, certain people can be trusted, and under the right circumstances, the group can be trusted.

We don't have to keep endeavoring to win the war on our own. A "support group" is meant to be just that: support. It carries within itself the idea of giving assistance, offering compassion, upholding, and encouraging someone to stay on the pathway that leads to life and freedom. That kind of support tells us, and shows us, that we no longer have to go through life alone.

I wasn't quite sure what to do with that truth, but I learned that part of the recovery process involves opening my mind and heart to receive. It involves letting other people in, and oftentimes, letting God in. I didn't realize I was holding God at arm's length, but much of the time, I was. I intellectually acknowledged Him as God, but I didn't embrace Him as the loving, trustworthy Father. Throughout this process, we often find it necessary to examine what we actually believe and then assess if we are really walking in true faith or not. These are tough questions that require the presence and help of other people who have walked the pathway before us. They know that it's hard. But they also know that the path gets easier as you continue to put one foot in front of the other with someone walking beside you. We were not meant to travel through this life as a "one-man band," isolated in our pain and in our efforts to be rid of the pain. So, anytime we choose to yield and receive, there is natural and supernatural assistance available to jointly shoulder the burden. And also share the joy.

Besides ... there is great wisdom waiting for us when we are humble enough to listen.

Recovery comes from the very heart of God, and the Steps are accomplished only through the power of God. So, I have found that it's extremely helpful to listen to how other people have connected with God and have worked the Steps themselves. I don't need to invent the wheel again; I can learn from their experience. The experience shared by others becomes my practical application.

After listening, I then put effort into learning to think and act in new and different ways. And constant reminders are needed to reinforce that new way of processing and behaving. If I don't have consistent reinforcement, it's easy to go back into my default mode, which is my old, insane way of trying to live life. So, I listen and learn, and listen and learn, and listen and learn. And then I apply, apply, apply. It's necessary to take action.

But action that is taken then becomes experience that can be shared.

This element of learning from one another is one of the most beautiful things to me about support groups. Somehow it seems to reflect the core and essence of God. We are all unique and valuable, and each of us can be used by God to touch the lives of others, no matter where we are in our recovery. The truth you have found, whether it be great or small, may be just the word that someone else needs to hear. Even a total newcomer who has just found hope has something to share. So, in the end, our support groups are sustained by those who are finding freedom through the power of God, and who understand that in order to keep that freedom ... it must be given away. Sometimes we share the experience of what doesn't work and how that pushed us to try things in a different way to find out what does work. If we share our weaknesses and testify how God, through the Steps, brought us to a place of positive change, then we have shared something of great value. And that's how I see the dynamics of a support group.

In the preamble that is often read at the beginning of AA meetings, it says, "Alcoholics Anonymous is a fellowship of men and women who share their experience, strength, and hope with each other that they may solve their common problem and help others to recover from alcoholism."[41]

What a beautiful concept. We stand with each other in unity, compassion, and genuine love because that is the support we offer, and that is the support that works for those who choose to work it.

Another wonderful benefit that comes from sharing our stories is the opportunity to release our pain ... pain that most of us have lived with for a lifetime. The truth is, God did not equip us to carry chronic emotional pain. We will falter under its weight and be crippled by it if we try; a solemn fact to which many of us can testify. Jesus came to heal the brokenhearted and is truly committed to our wholeness, so He offers us many ways to deal with pain. Probably the biggest, most effective option is to learn to trust God. We make the choice to give our wills and our lives over to His care. But trust is a choice, and trust is learned through repeated experience, so some of us aren't ready to do that the moment we walk through the recovery door. We can, however, sometimes begin by trusting the unity of the group, or by trusting a friend, and we can learn to trust our sponsor.

A sponsor is someone with a track record of recovery who helps us learn how to walk through the Twelve Steps. They help us personalize those Steps until they become our own. They guide; they listen; they encourage; they suggest; they offer different perspectives; and they care. They also might point us to reading materials that will help, or to listening materials that will inspire. They commit themselves to praying for us. A sponsor is also someone who, with our permission, helps us identify a character defect, or where, how, and why we might be stumbling. We all need someone like that. Sponsors do all these things because they know how beneficial it is to keep the message going.

But we must also understand that, even though a sponsor will come alongside us and provide specific support, they are not equipped to "save" us from our pain any more than we are equipped to save ourselves. Only Jesus is equipped to do that. So, please keep in mind that people can hear our pain, and that can be helpful, but only God can actually heal it. No matter where we initially take our pain, my prayer is that we will eventually go to the One who has the power and desire to take the pain away.

History shows that support groups have proved to be highly successful in helping people recover from their addictive tendencies. And because of that, it's vitally important to protect the unity and strength of the group. God patented this design. But even though we have the group for support, we need to also remember that this Program stems from our individual free-will. The choice is ours and ours alone. We can choose to go forward; we can choose to stop; or we can choose to never get started at all. As they say: recovery isn't for those who need it, it's for those who want it. We have to want recovery bad enough to work the Steps and to apply the principles in our daily lives. That's where readiness comes in and where choice becomes primary. It takes work, and anyone who is in active recovery will confirm that it takes work. But that's okay.

... The results are no less than miraculous.

The Twelve Steps[42] and Corresponding Bible Verses

1. **We admitted we were powerless over alcohol (our addictions), and that our lives had become unmanageable.** "*I don't really understand myself, for I want to do what is right, but I don't do it.... And I know that nothing good lives in me... I want to do what is right, but I can't*" (Romans 7:15, 18, NLT). "*Jesus replied, 'I tell you the truth, everyone who sins is a slave of sin*'" (John 8:34, NLT).

2. **Came to believe that a Power greater than ourselves could restore us to sanity.** "*For God is working in you, giving you the desire and the power to do what pleases Him*" (Philippians 2:13, NLT). "*O Sovereign Lord! You made the heavens and earth by your strong hand and powerful arm. Nothing is too hard for You*" (Jeremiah 32:17, NLT). "*... The Lord is the everlasting God, the Creator of all the earth... He gives power to the weak and strength to the powerless*" (Isaiah 40:28,29, NLT).

3. **Made a decision to turn our will and our lives over to the care of God.** *"And so, dear brothers and sisters, I plead with you to give your bodies to God because of all he has done for you. Let them be a living and holy sacrifice—the kind he will find acceptable"* (Romans 12:1, NLT). *"Then Jesus said, 'Come to me, all of you who are weary and carry heavy burdens, and I will give you rest. Take my yoke upon you. Let me teach you, because I am humble and gentle at heart, and you will find rest for your souls. For my yoke is easy to bear, and the burden I give you is light'"* (Matthew 11: 28–30, NLT). *"Jesus said, 'The food that keeps me going is that I do the will of the One who sent me, finishing the work he started'"* (John 4:34, MSG).

4. **Made a searching and fearless moral inventory of ourselves.** *"Instead, let us test and examine our ways. Let us turn back to the Lord"* (Lamentations 3:40, NLT). *"Search me, O God, and know my heart; test me and know my anxious thoughts. Point out anything in me that offends you, and lead me along the path of everlasting life"* (Psalm 139:23–24, NLT).

5. **Admitted to God, to ourselves, and to another human being the exact nature of our wrongs.** *"Confess your sins to each other and pray for each other so that you may be healed"* (James 5:16, NLT). *"When I refused to confess my sin, my body wasted away, and I groaned all day long.... Finally, I confessed all my sins to you and stopped trying to hide my guilt. I said to myself, 'I will confess my rebellion to the Lord.' And you forgave me! All my guilt is gone"* (Psalm 32:3,5, NLT).

6. **Were entirely ready to have God remove all these defects of character.** *"Humble yourselves before the Lord, and he will lift you up in honor"* (James 4:10, NLT). *"So humble yourselves under the mighty power of God, and at the right time he will lift you up in honor. Give all your worries and cares to God, for he cares about you"* (1 Peter 5:6–7, NLT).

7. **Humbly asked Him to remove our shortcomings.** *"But if we confess our sins to him, he is faithful and just to forgive us our sins and to cleanse us from all wickedness"* (1 John 1:9, NLT). *"... And the Lord— who is the Spirit—makes us more and more like him as we are changed into his glorious image"* (2 Corinthians 3:18, NLT).

8. **Made of list of all persons we had harmed and became willing to make amends to them all.** *"Do to others as you would like them to do to you"* (Luke 6:31, NLT). *"Dear children, let's not merely say that we love each other; let us show the truth by our actions"* (1 John 3:18, NLT).

9. **Made direct amends to such people wherever possible, except when to do so would injure them or others.** *"So, if you are presenting a sacrifice at the altar and ... someone has something against you, leave your sacrifice there at the altar. Go and be reconciled to that person. Then come and offer your sacrifice to God"* (Matthew 5:23–24, NLT). *"For God called you to do good, even if it means suffering, just as Christ suffered for you. He is your example, and you must follow in his steps. He never sinned, nor ever deceived anyone. He did not retaliate when he was insulted, nor threaten revenge when he suffered. He left his case in the hands of God, who always judges fairly"* (1 Peter 2:21–23, NLT).

10. **Continued to take personal inventory and, when we were wrong, promptly admitted it.** *"If you think you are standing strong, be careful not to fall"* (1 Corinthians 10:12, NLT). *"If we claim we have no sin, we are only fooling ourselves and not living in the truth"* (1 John 1:8, NLT). *"Examine yourselves to see if your faith is genuine. Test yourselves"* (2 Corinthians 13:5, NLT).

11. **Sought through prayer and meditation to improve our conscious contact with God, praying only for knowledge of His will for us and the power to carry that out.** *"Devote yourselves to prayer with an alert mind and a thankful heart"* (Colossians 4:2, NLT). *"Yes, I am the vine; you are the branches. Those who remain in me, and I in them, will produce much fruit. For apart from me you can do nothing"* (John 15:5, NLT). *"I will study your commandments and reflect on your ways. I will delight in your decrees and not forget your word"* (Psalm 119:15–16, NLT).

12. **Having had a spiritual awakening as the result of these Steps, we tried to carry this message to those still suffering and to practice these principles in all our affairs.** *"The Spirit of the Sovereign Lord is upon me, for the Lord anointed me to bring good news to the poor. He has sent me to comfort the brokenhearted and to proclaim that captives will be released and prisoners will be freed"* (Isaiah 61:1, NLT). *"Once we, too, were foolish and disobedient. We were misled and became slaves to many lusts and pleasures. Our lives were full of evil and envy, and we hated each other. But, when God our Savior revealed his kindness and love, he saved us, not because of the righteous things we had done, but because of his mercy. He washed away our sins, giving us a new birth and new life through the Holy Spirit"* (Titus 3:3–5, NLT).

Bibliography

Alcoholics Anonymous, 3rd Edition. New York: Alcoholics Anonymous World Services, Inc., 1939, 1955, 1976.

Beattie, Melody. *Codependent No More*. New York: Harper & Row, Publishers, Inc., by arrangement with the Hazelden Foundation, 1987.

Beattie, Melody. *The Language of Letting Go*. New York: HarperCollins Publishers, by arrangement with the Hazelden Foundation, 1990.

Cruz, Nicky with Buckingham, Jamie. *Run Baby Run*. Plainfield, New Jersey: Logos Books, 1970.

Lawrence, Marc. *Two Weeks Notice*. Theatrical film version. Directed by Marc Lawrence. Los Angeles: Warner Bros., 2002.

Meyer, Joyce. *Battlefield of the Mind*. New York: Warner Books, Inc., 1995.

Meyer, Joyce. *The Root of Rejection*. Tulsa, Oklahoma: Harrison House, 1994.

Platt, Emily. "Gerald McRaney of 'This Is Us' Proposed to Wife Delta Burke on Their Second Date." *Martha Stewart Weddings*, 11 Sept. 2017, marthastewart.com/7903813/ gerald-mcraney-delta-burke-proposal-story.

Subby, Robert and Friel, John. *Codependency, An Emerging Issue*. Unknown place of publication: Health Communications, 1983. Quoted in Melody Beattie, *Codependent No More*. New York: Harper & Row, Publishers, Inc., by arrangement with the Hazelden Foundation, 1987.

Twelve Steps and Twelve Traditions. New York: The A.A. Grapevine, Inc., and Alcoholics Anonymous World Services, Inc., 1952, 1953, 1981.

Wikipedia. "Oxford Group." Last modified September 11, 2021. https://en.wikipedia.org/wiki/Oxford_Group.

About the Author

KIM SON HAS BEEN DEDI-CATED to Christian ministry for over forty years as a teacher, writer, worship leader, and former co-pastor. After struggling for decades with food addiction and codependency, rooted in a family history of alcoholism, Kim now communicates a message of God's incredible power to heal. She shares a pathway to freedom that was inspired and propelled by His unconditional love and His deep desire to see His children whole. To that end, she continues to reach out to those seeking recovery through her blog, *The Compulsive Cookie*. Between the two, Kim and her husband, Kenny, have four children and seven grandchildren, and live in the farm and ranch country of rural Kansas. She has a great love of family, horses, American history, and the unique beauty of her native state which she captures through her artwork. For more information, see Kim's website at: www.mkimson.com.

Endnotes

1   *Two Weeks Notice,* directed by Marc Lawrence (2002; Los Angeles, CA: Warner Bros.), performances by Sandra Bullock and Hugh Grant, Theatrical Film Version.

2   *Alcoholics Anonymous,* (New York, Alcoholics Anonymous World Services, Inc., 1976), 58-59.

3   *Alcoholics Anonymous,* 58.

4   Robert Subby and John Friel, *Co-dependency, An Emerging Issue,* (Unknown place of publication, Health Communications, 1983), 31, quoted in Melody Beattie, *Codependent No More,* (New York, Harper & Row, Publishers, Inc., by arrangement with the Hazelden Foundation, 1987), 29.

5   Melody Beattie, *Codependent No More,* (New York, Harper & Row, Publishers, Inc., by arrangement with the Hazelden Foundation, 1987).

6   Emily Platt, "Gerald McRaney of 'This Is Us' Proposed to Wife Delta Burke on Their Second Date." *Martha Stewart*

Weddings, Sept. 11, 2017, marthastewart.com/7903813/ gerald-mcraney-delta-burke-proposal-story.

7   *Alcoholics Anonymous*, 59-60.

8   *Alcoholics Anonymous*, 85.

9   *Twelve Steps and Twelve Traditions*, (New York, Alcoholics Anonymous World Services, Inc., 1981), 21.

10 Beattie, *Codependent No More*.

11 Origin Unknown. Slogan used with permission from Alcoholics Anonymous World Services, Inc.

12 *Twelve Steps and Twelve Traditions*, 25.

13 Merriam-Webster, s.v. "sanity," accessed February 16, 2020, http://www.merriam-webster.com/sanity.

14 "Oxford Group," Wikipedia, last modified September 11, 2021, https://en.wikipedia.org/wiki/Oxford_Group.

15 *Alcoholics Anonymous*, 83-84.

16 *Twelve Steps and Twelve Traditions*, 34.

17 Melody Beattie, *The Language of Letting Go*, (New York, HarperCollins Publishers, by arrangement with the Hazelden Foundation, 1990), 129.

18 Nicky Cruz with Jamie Buckingham, *Run Baby Run*, (Plainfield, New Jersey, Logos Books, 1970)

19 Merriam-Webster, s.v. "process," accessed March 2, 2020, http://www.merriam-webster.com/process.

20 *Twelve Steps and Twelve Traditions*, 42.

21 *Alcoholics Anonymous*, 58.

22 *Twelve Steps and Twelve Traditions*, 55.

23 *Twelve Steps and Twelve Traditions*, 63.

24 *Twelve Steps and Twelve Traditions*, 70.

25 *Twelve Steps and Twelve Traditions*, 76.

26 *Twelve Steps and Twelve Traditions*, 77.

27 Joyce Meyer, *The Root of Rejection*, (Tulsa, Oklahoma, Harrison House, 1994), 43.

28 *Alcoholics Anonymous*, 449.

29 *Twelve Steps and Twelve Traditions*, 83.

30 Vocabulary (online dictionary), s.v. "absolve," accessed October 2, 2021, http://www.vocabulary.com/dictionary/absolve.

31 *Alcoholics Anonymous*, 85.

32 *Twelve Steps and Twelve Traditions*, 88.

33 Joyce Meyer, *Battlefield of the Mind*, (New York, Warner Books, Inc., 1995), 66.

34 *Twelve Steps and Twelve Traditions*, 96.

35 *Alcoholics Anonymous*, 58-59.

36 *Twelve Steps and Twelve Traditions*, 106.

37 *Alcoholics Anonymous*, xv-xvi (Forward to Second Edition).

38 *Alcoholics Anonymous*, 83-84.

39 AA Motto, origin unknown.

40 *Alcoholics Anonymous*, 59.

41 A.A. Preamble, opening statement.

42 *Alcoholics Anonymous*, 59-60.

Printed in Great Britain
by Amazon

16718613R00160